Davie Armstrong: A Story Of The Fells

Austin Clare

DAVIE ARMSTRONG.

A STORY OF THE FELLS.

By AUSTIN CLARE,

Author of "*André's Trial.*"

PUBLISHED UNDER THE DIRECTION OF
THE COMMITTEE OF GENERAL LITERATURE AND EDUCATION
APPOINTED BY THE SOCIETY FOR PROMOTING
CHRISTIAN KNOWLEDGE.

LONDON:
SOCIETY FOR PROMOTING CHRISTIAN KNOWLEDGE.
SOLD AT THE DEPOSITORIES:
77 GREAT QUEEN STREET, LINCOLN'S INN FIELDS;
4 ROYAL EXCHANGE; 48 PICCADILLY;
AND BY ALL BOOKSELLERS.

1489. f 588.

"Lead us not into temptation; But deliver us from evil."

"Thou didst foil the Tempter's power,
Help me in temptation's hour."
Mrs. Alexander.

TO MY FATHER AND MOTHER.

Page 11.

DAVIE ARMSTRONG.

CHAPTER I.

A WILD NIGHT'S RIDE.

THE afternoon sun was fast disappearing
behind a thick curtain of grey cloud; its
parting rays shone with a stormy light
over the landscape, tinting with fresh colour
the weather-stained ruins of Penrith Castle
and the old houses built of the red free-
stone * from which the town takes its name.
There was a raw, biting chill in the air,
and a threatening look in the sky, which
made the market-people glance upwards, and
then quicken their homeward-bound steps,
in anticipation of a storm. The market had

* _Pen_ and _rhudd_ signify, in the British language, _red_
hill.

not lasted long that day, for it was much too
cold to stand bargaining and chaffering in
the open air; and now, though it was only
between three and four o'clock, the market-
place was well-nigh deserted, with the exception of a few stall-keepers, who remained
to pack up their wares; and some country-
folk from a distance, who were standing
about the inn-doors, muffling themselves in
their plaids, and waiting for their respective
horses to be brought out. Among these last
was a lad of some sixteen or seventeen years,
who stood with his hand on the shaggy mane
of a rough, sturdy little fell-pony, waiting
till it should have finished munching the last
grains from a bag of oats, which was hanging under its nose. Meanwhile, the last of
the farmers rode off, and the jolly landlord
came to the doorway, and stood looking after
them, with his hands in his pockets. "Well,
my lad," he said presently, turning to the
boy, " better not think of crossing the fell
to-night, it'll be snow long afore ye get to

Alston; stay and put up wi' me." "No,
thank ye, maister, I maun be off, they'll be
lookin' for me at hame." "Well, I wouldn't
try, if I were you; d'ye see that cloud atop
o' Cross Fell? the Helm Wind 'll be on, afore
long, or I'm much mistaken. Think better
on't, Davie, and bide till the morn." Davie
laughed. "No, no, I maun be off, I'll be on
t' other side o' the fell, long afore the storm
breaks!" "Where ye ever out in t' Helm?"
"No, but I've been out in many a storm
afore now, and I'm not afraid." Saying
which, Davie leapt on his pony's back,
gathered up the reins, and with a cheery
"good-day," trotted off at a brisk pace.
The landlord scratched his nose, and uttered
a long whistle. "Eh, well!" he muttered,
turning indoors, "that's a lad that won't
hear reason; I only hope he'll come to no
harm, for it'll be a wild night. Eh, well!
'he that wull to Cupar, maun to Cupar,' as
they say, t' other side o' the Border." With
these words, the jolly landlord shut out the

cold air, and betook himself to his pipe in the warm bar.

But we must follow Davie, cold though it be, for it is with his fortunes that we have to do. Let me introduce him to you, as he sits on his shaggy pony, trotting away at such a steady pace, along the high road.

Davie Armstrong was a Northumbrian born and bred; tall and strong like most of his race, with curly hair, wavering between red and brown; honest grey eyes, in which lurked the spirits—good or otherwise, according as they are curbed, or allowed to run riot — of independence, determination, and fearless love of adventure. His skin, originally fair, was tanned and browned with exposure to the sun and wind; and his whole appearance had a pleasant air of free activity and strong, healthy vigour. He wore a shepherd's plaid over his rough homespun suit, and a Scotch bonnet on his curly head.

Davie had other reasons, than he had thought fit to confide to the landlord, for

wishing to return home that night; he had
been sent over to Penrith by a Northumbrian
farmer, to whom he was shepherd, to receive
the price of some sheep which had been sold
the week before, and his master had charged
him on no account to remain in the town
over-night. For some time, boy and pony
travelled on without any interruption, for,
though the wind was raw and cold, it was
not high, and Davie was too well accustomed
to be out in all weathers, to mind having his
hair tossed about a little, and his hands
chilled with its breath. The clouds, indeed,
were gradually becoming darker and heavier,
but while the slanting rays of the sun still
shone out fitfully from below them, Davie
would not give up the hope that the landlord's prophesy would prove to be a false one.

"Come on, Meg, my lass, thou shalt have
a bit o' oat-cake if thou canst win hame afore
the storm breaks," he said, patting Meg's
tangled mane encouragingly; and the little
pony pricked up its ears, and trotted on faster

than ever, through the richly-cultivated country which surrounds Penrith like a garden,
and which, even on that stormy February day,
offered a striking contrast to the rugged
mountains which looked down upon it, in
their grim garniture of trailing cloud, dark
withered heather, and grey rock. On trotted
Meg, clattering through pretty villages
nestled among old trees, where the lights
were beginning to peep from each cottage
window, and the fire-light shone cheerily
out into the fast gathering twilight. Davie
thought of the warm fire-side at home, and
Meg probably thought of her comfortable
stable, for the little hoofs beat quicker time
on the hard road, striking out flashes of fire
as they clattered over the stones. Leaving
the region of hedge-rows behind them, they
came to where rough stone walls shut in the
road, and presently, as they began to ascend
the steep declivity of Hartside, even these
tokens of civilisation were left in the rear,
and the road wound up the open fell, with no

boundary but a row of white posts painted
black at the top, placed at regular intervals
along one side, as a guide to travellers journey-
ing through the snow. It was growing very
dark, and what there was to be seen, was of
the most dreary and desolate description.
Dark mountains frowned out of the gloom on
every side; cold grey blocks of limestone
cropped up from among the withered heather,
looking almost phantom-like in the twilight;
a few horned mountain sheep wandered rest-
lessly about, bleating piteously; and the wind
moaned among the brown bent, dying away
for a moment, and then rising again in a low
sob of almost human misery. Presently a
snowflake settled like a white feather on
Davie's plaid; he brushed it hastily away,
and began whistling "The Girl I left behind
me;" but, as though the snow were determined not to be ignored, another flake fell,
and yet another, till the black checkers in
Davie's plaid disappeared entirely, under a
soft cover of downy white. There was now

no-doubt of the matter,—he was fairly in for
a snow-storm, and a snow-storm is no light
thing on those wild open fells, with no human
habitation within many miles: so, though
Davie continued to whistle away as vigorously
as ever, he began to feel a little uncomfortable
when he thought of the long distance which
was still between him and his home.   He
chirped to Meg, but Meg was already going as
fast as she could, and, moreover, found the
uphill road, with the snow driving in her face,
remarkably tiring.   They were still a good
half mile from the top of the mountain pass,
when Meg suddenly pricked up her ears,
started, and began to tremble violently.
Hark! what was it?—that distant noise, like
the roar of artillery, coming nearer and nearer
down the fell?—Davie had no need to ask
himself this question; *he* knew only too well
what it was, for he had heard it many a time
before, when safe out of its reach in his own
valley,—it was the terrible Helm Wind.[b]

[b] A hurricane peculiar to this range of mountains; so

His heart beat a little faster, but he only
pulled his bonnet over his eyes, tightened his
hold on Meg's reins, and moved slowly forwards. On came the wind, rushing through
the crevices of the mountains, with a sound
like thunder, and driving the snow before it
in blinding showers: terrible was the shock
with which it met the living obstacle in its
headlong career; poor little Meg was blown
completely round, and her master, gasping for
breath, was obliged to dismount, and turn
his back on the wind, to recover himself in
some measure, before endeavouring to force
his way onward to some place of shelter; for
it was impossible to remain where he was,
exposed to the full fury of the hurricane on
the open fell-side. He knew that if he could
once get a certain distance down the opposite
side of the mountain, he should be beyond

called from a cloud on the summit of Cross Fell, in shape
like a helmet, from which it issues, rushing down the
western side of the mountain with terrific force. It is
most frequent in spring and autumn. Similar winds
are known at the Cape of Good Hope, Mont Cenis,
Trieste, &c.

the limits of the wind, which only blows
within a certain area; but how to achieve
this was the difficulty. Meg was nearly wild
with terror, and made frantic efforts to get
loose, and rush back again down the hill;
and Davie, strong as he was, found it almost
beyond his power to hold her in, and at the
same time to make way in the teeth of that
mighty wind, which raged and roared, as
though the demons of the storm had escaped
from the power of the Cross, under which,
according to tradition, S. Augustine had
bound them, and had once more taken pos-
session of their old haunts.[c]   But Davie was
not a boy to be easily beaten; slowly but
surely he advanced, one step at a time, en-
couraging Meg with voice and hand, turning
round every now and then to take breath, and

c "Cross Fell is said to have been formerly designated
Fiend's Fell, from the common belief that evil spirits had
their haunt upon it, until S. Augustine erected a *Cross*,
and built an altar on the summit, where he offered the
Holy Eucharist, and thus countercharmed the demons.
Since that time it has borne the name of Cross Fell."
—Black's *English Lakes*.

then struggling on again, with his head bent,
and the pony's bridle wound round his arm.
Thus with great difficulty he succeeded in
reaching the head of the pass; but once there
he could get no farther. The wind had risen
to a terrific height, and swept round the
corner in fierce, wild blasts, whirling the snow
round and round, and drifting it in long
white wreaths across the road. Giddy and
bewildered, Davie felt that he must give in,
—he had been struggling bravely with the
storm for the last half hour, but his strength
was well-nigh exhausted, and his breath was
almost gone. What was to be done?—The
boy stood for a moment, clinging to the pony,
and trying to think; but it was hard work
in the midst of that wild uproar: think he
must, however, for he well knew that, if once
he lost his head, all would be over with him.
Suddenly a bright thought struck him; he
remembered that somewhere round the corner,
on the right-hand side of the road, the ground
sloped down abruptly, forming a deep hollow

between two hills; once gain this, and he
would be in comparative shelter. Turning
his back to the wind, he drew a long breath,
and struggled on once more. How he found
the place, and scrambled down the bank,
Davie hardly knew, till he found himself
sitting, panting and exhausted, between the
side of the hill and a great white snowdrift,
which effectually screened him from the
violence of the storm. Poor little Meg was
standing beside him, trembling in every limb,
and breathing hard. The lad stroked her
quivering nostrils,—" Never mind, Meg, my
lass; we'll get home all right, sometime."—
Sometime, yes; but how and when? Davie
began to have uncomfortable recollections of
gruesome stories he had heard,—stories which
told of men overtaken by snow-storms on
these very fells, who had sunk down exhausted, and had fallen into a deadly sleep to
wake no more; men who had left their homes
brave and well, as he had done, never to
return again, but as corpses, stiff and frozen

by just such a terrible wind as was moaning
and howling round his place of refuge. It
was an awful thought; Davie did not like it,
and shook himself impatiently, but it was of
no use, the thoughts were not to be shaken
off so easily, and they soon came back again.
What if such were to be his fate? He pictured the grief of his old grandparents, on
seeing the last of their children, their only
remaining stay, carried home stiff and cold:
he thought of his dog, his dear old Laddie,
who had guided him faithfully through many
a storm; what would *he* do, if his young
master were to be brought home dead? *Dead!*
the word made him shudder; how was he fit
to meet this death, this terrible death?

Now Davie was not exactly a bad boy, but
neither was he a very good one. He had
been carefully taught and prepared for his
Confirmation; but during the year which had
passed since that, he had led a very careless
life; with school and catechising he had
thrown off a good deal of the restraint of

c

outward observances, had got into bad company, been irregular in his attendance at
church, had often forgotten his daily prayers;
and though he had not yet been guilty of any
open sin, his life had been very far from what
it should be. He thought of this now;
thought of it rather with fear, than with any
great sorrow for what had been amiss;
thought of it, till the thought of death and
punishment grew so great, he could bear it
no longer. He knelt down and tried to
pray; but he was so bewildered, he could
think of nothing, and a dark dread came over
him that he had no right to expect help, he
had forgotten God when all went well, and
how could he hope He would remember him
now? But God had not forgotten him,
erring sheep though he was, and He brought
back a long neglected prayer to the lad's
mind, beautiful words from our Church's
Liturgy; happy they who have learnt her
prayers, and to whose memory they come
back in the dark hour when the mind is

too bewildered to find words for itself:—
"Almighty and everlasting God, mercifully
look upon our infirmities, and in all our
dangers and necessities stretch forth Thy
right hand to help and defend us; through
Jesus Christ our Lord. Amen." Davie said
the words over several times, and by degrees
the fear passed away, the dark dread lifted
itself from his mind, and he was himself
again. Standing up, he stamped his feet
vigorously on the ground, and struck his
crossed arms over his breast, to keep off the
numbness that was creeping over him; then
he spoke to Meg, patted her drooping head,
and sitting down, he made himself as comfortable as the circumstances permitted, drew
his plaid over his head, and waited in hopes
that the storm would subside sufficiently to
allow of his taking the road again. Presently
an avalanche of snow fell down on his head
from the bank above; there was a sound of
something trying to retain foothold, then a
crash, a sharp cry, and a heavy body rolled

down, and lay motionless at Davie's feet.
The lad started up. " I say, wha's there ?"
No answer. Davie went nearer, and touched
the prostrate form. " Wha's there? Can't
ye speak ?" " Oh, dinna hurt me, dinna
hurt me !" answered a low frightened voice,
scarcely audible in the storm. " Hurt ye?
I'm not going to hurt ye," replied Davie
impatiently, " what gars (*makes*) ye think
that? Can't ye tell me what they call ye?"
" Willie Kirk," answered the voice, in a
somewhat less frightened tone. " Oh, aye, I
know," returned Davie; " ye live in Alston,
and go wi' t' waggons in one o' the mines at
Neuthead?" " Aye." " And how is't ye're
here ?" " Ou, I was just goin' over to
Melmerby when t' wind caught me, and blew
me clean over t' bank side." " Just so,"
replied Davie, sententiously; " well, ye can't
get over to Melmerby to-night, onyhow, so
ye'd better turn round an' go back along wi'
me. The wind's not that high now, and as
there're two of us, I ken a way'll hinder us

losing the road." "Oh, aye, I'll go back wi'
ye," assented Willie, "I daren't go on alone,
in sich a flow (*stormy*) night." Accordingly,
after the new-comer was sufficiently rested,
Davie proceeded to carry out his plan.
Stationing Willie at the nearest snow-post,
he bade him continue shouting as loud as he
could, while he and Meg went forward to the
next, which—being aided by the sound to
keep in a straight line—he managed to reach
without much difficulty. Arrived there,
Davie stopped, and began shouting in his
turn, and Willie, guided by his voice, soon
came up with him. Thus they went on,
riding Meg, turn and turn about, till, after a
long and weary time, the sight of lights at
the foot of the hill told them that they were
once more in a land inhabited. After crossing the bridge over the Tyne, the two lads
parted company, Willie betaking himself to
his abode in an unsavoury part of Alston,
termed the "Butts," while Davie proceeded to
his home in the adjoining county. The storm

was now over, so that all further danger
was at an end, and, had it not been for the
deep snow which covered the road, Meg would
soon have accomplished the three miles which
lay between her and home. As it was, it
was late when they crossed the bridge over
the Ayle Burn, which here forms the boundary between Cumberland and Northum-
berland; so late, that every light was out in
the village of Ayle, where Davie's master
lived, and he had to go straight home
without delivering up his money.

CHAPTER II.

DAVIE AT HOME.

It stood on the hill-side, that home, which had been the subject of the ardent longings of both Meg and her master, during all those long hours of storm and darkness. It was a humble little cottage enough, with white-washed walls, and gray slated roof tacked down to the said walls with great iron stitches, as a precaution against the wind, which otherwise might have carried it off bodily many a time, so exposed was the little building to every gale, except that which blew from the north-west, and against this the steep, sloping side of Ayle Fell formed an efficient protection. Underneath its sturdy shelter nestled a tiny garden, where gooseberry and currant-bushes flourished in the proper season, and the rosy-stalked rhubarb uncurled its crumpled leaves. But humble as it was, this little cottage had one advantage for which the possessors of many a grander mansion might well have envied it—a magnificent view; a view of coppice, river, and hill, with white-capped Cross Fell frowning high above them all in the far distance.

But we are leaving Davie in the cold all this time, though you may be pretty sure he did not wait for us there, but, after carefully ensconcing Meg in the stable, which she shared with a highly respectable black cow, and duly providing for her comfort, he turned his steps towards the cottage door.

"Oh, my lad, my lad, so ye're here at last, and the storm hasna kilt ye!" was the exclamation with which he was greeted on entering the house; "I've been awful frightened that I'd never see ye again. Eh, but I *have* suffered; ye can hae nae idea what I

hae gone through! Eh, but sich anxiety is
bad for me i' my weak state o' health!"
The speaker,—an old woman, wearing a dark
stuff gown, and a large white cap, so closely
plaited around her face, as almost entirely
to conceal the grey hair underneath,—possessed the talent of lamentation in‾ a high
degree, which, together with the gift of a
plaintive voice, enabled her so to magnify
the evils of a slightly delicate constitu-
tion, that any one unacquainted with this
peculiarity would have imagined her sufferings to be unparalleled. Davie answered his
grandmother rather unceremoniously, and
began shaking the snow from his plaid; but
the dame, indignant at having her sufferings thus lightly esteemed, burst out with
a stream of complaints. "An' what for
did Tom Reed send ye to Pe'rith in sich
weather? He should consider afore he sends
a lad who's the only stay o' twa puir auld
folks, over the fells, where he might have
been lost in the storm as easy as onything;

it isna richt, that it isn't. And ye, too, lad
what gar'd (*made*) ye come hame sae late?
There's the puir auld man, yer grandfather,
was sair put about for ye; he wanted to sit
up till ye came, but I wadna hear on't, bad
as he is wi' the rheumatics. When will the
day come when ye'll consider his sufferings?
—and mine too,—is it richt for a weakly
body like me to be sittin' up till this time o'
night, think ye?"

Davie was now thoroughly out of humour.
His grandmother's lamentations had seemed
to him pathetic enough in imagination, when
he had pictured himself being carried home
dead; but now that that tragic possibility
was over, when he had come home, not frozen
and motionless, but only very tired and cold,
and most unromantically hungry and cross,
the reality was so far from touching him,
that it irritated him beyond endurance.

"Hout, granny! what's the use of makin'
sich a rout about nothin'? Do haud yer
tongue, and get me some supper." The old

woman looked hurt and grieved; she was really
fond of the lad, and all this lamentation and
complaint was owing to the anxiety she had
felt for his safety. It was her way of unbur-
dening her mind, but it had a very bad effect
on a boy of Davie's character. " Ay, ay, that's
always the way," she murmured, half crying,
"a body may wear theirsels to bits for a heed-
less lad, and a' the thanks they get is hard
words." She set a bowl of smoking porridge
on the table, made up the fire, and retired
into the inner room, with her apron to her
eyes. Davie sat still in the ingle-nook,
where he had placed himself on first entering,
staring into the fire, and leaving his porridge
untouched. He was sorry for having spoken
so crossly to his grandmother, though his
pride would not let him show it, so long as
she remained in the room. How long he
would have sat there I do not know, probably
till the quietness of the little room and the
heat of the fire had sent him to sleep, but he
was soon disturbed by a cold nose being

thrust into his hand, and looking up, he saw
a great shaggy shepherd's dog, using every
effort to attract his attention. "Laddie,
poor old boy, is it you?" he said, stroking
the creature's soft head. "So, ho! it's supper-
time, is it? Well, come along, old lad."
Davie and his dog always shared the evening's bowl of porridge between them, and
Laddie evidently had no idea that this night
should prove an exception to the general
rule, though I am by no means sure that he
had not supped long before his master came
in. The porridge disposed of, Davie climbed
wearily up the ladder to the loft which served
him as a sleeping-room, threw off his clothes,
and utterly forgetful of the thanks which were
due to his Almighty Father, for bringing
him safely through that terrible storm, he
scrambled into bed, and fell asleep immediately.

Does this shock you very much? Are you
surprised that Davie should so soon have
forgotten all that he had gone through that

very evening? I am afraid that it is nothing
very unusual: he had not been really sorry
for his faults; they had risen up before him
in the hour of danger, and had filled him
with fear, but that was all; the danger past,
he fell back all too readily into his old ways.
When our feet once begin to stray from the
narrow road, it is by no means easy to retrace
our steps.

CHAPTER III.

BONNIE BELL.

Next morning Davie was up betimes, and set off to take his master the price of the sheep. It was a fine frosty morning; the newly-fallen snow lay pure and stainless over field and fell, glittering in the rays of the rising sun, which rose gloriously over the white mountains, making the opposite summits flush into tender rose-colour, like miniature Alps, against their stainless background of cloudless blue. As Davie and his dog sprang briskly over the last stile, they came face to face with a tall, powerfully-built old man with grizzled hair, and face still fresh and ruddy in spite of the furrows and weather-marks of more than sixty years. It was

Thomas Reed, Davie's master. "Well, Davie, my lad," he exclaimed, in a strong, hearty voice, bringing his heavy right hand down on the boy's shoulder, "safe home, eh? That's right; I was just coming to see after ye; the bairn couldn't rest for thinking ye might be lying under the snow-wreaths atop o' Hartside. I told her Davie Armstrong wasn't the lad to lose himself so easily, but the little lass wouldn't let me rest till I came to see. Ha, ha! lasses are wilful hussies,— they *will* have their way, as you'll find out to your cost one day, Davie, lad. And you've not lost my siller in the hullabulloo last night? No? That's right; you're a downright brave lad, Davie, I would trust you where I wouldn't trust a man twice your age. But you must have had a hard pull to get through last night. Here,—you shan't have cause to say Tom Reed doesn't know a good servant when he's got one (he pressed half-a-crown into the lad's hand); come and take your tea with us to-night; the bairn'll be keen to know

how you and Meg managed in the snow.
That's right. Good day, my lad." " Good
day, sir, and thank ye, sir," exclaimed Davie,
turning homewards, in high glee at his
unexpected riches and his master's praise.

Sundown found our hero dressed in his best
on his way to the village of Ayle; but this
same village deserves a word or two. It
stood on the hill-side, and consisted of one
little straggling street, on each side of which
were grouped the houses in glorious indif-
ference as to size and regularity; here stood
three or four in a row, with the ground a
good deal cut up before them, by the depreda-
tions of pigs and chickens; there the school-
house, popped down by itself in front of all
the rest, like a naughty child in disgrace; and
behind it was the schoolmaster's pretty cottage, with honeysuckle looking in at the
upper windows.

The villagers seemed to take a pride in
keeping the interior of their houses the picture
of neatness; a Dutchman need not have been

ashamed of the clean stone floors, well-scoured
tables, and bright fire-sides; and, indeed, it
would have been a shame had it been otherwise, for water abounds in this hill-country; a
stream poured down the hill-side at the head
of the village-street, and another dashed in
miniature waterfalls through the rock-strewn
copse-wood at the foot. Here the village girls
might be seen with their water-cans morning
and evening, in their picturesque costume of
coloured print bed-gowns, with sleeves reaching to the elbow, and dark woollen petticoats,
short enough to give every advantage to a
trig ankle,—a costume, which, if they would
only believe it, is so much more becoming to
them than any other. Nearly all the villagers were *statesmen,* as the local term is;
that is to say, men living on and farming
their own little piece of land, which, in many
cases, has descended from father to son for
generations. Davie's master belonged to this
class, but his estate was larger than that of
any of his neighbours, and his house more

D

substantial and better built. It stood at the lower end of the village, a long building of grey stone, mellowed by time and tempest into a medley of a hundred blended tints; emerald moss cushioned the joinings of the slated roof, yellow lichen crept over the stone mullions of the latticed windows, and traced in gold the date, 1775, over the low doorway.

A pretty picture it was which presented itself to our friend Davie's eyes, as he opened that door on the evening in question. The low, wide kitchen was flooded with ruddy firelight, which basked on the flagged floor, and danced among the oaken rafters and their garniture of well-cured hams and flitches, suspended there with the master's old-fashioned gun and knotted walking-stick; warm light lit up the dark oak dresser, flickered merrily among the store of earthenware mugs and plates which adorned its shelves, and was flashed back in many a twinkling ray, from the rows of pewter pots, and the brass balls of the old eight-day clock which ticked contentedly in the corner, bearing on its face the perpetual image of the sun looking out from behind a cloud with an everlasting smile beaming from its placid features, made to represent those of the human face divine. On one side of the blazing fire sat the master in his armchair, his silver spectacles astride his nose, and a well-thumbed Prayer-book in his horny hand; while before him stood a lovely child of six or seven, with her chubby hands clasped together behind her back, repeating the lesson which was to be said in church at the catechising next Sunday. She wore a clean linen pinafore tied over her little frock of shepherd's plaid, and her fair, clustering curls hung in pretty confusion over her rosy face. Every now and then the little hands would unclasp, and one would steal down to pat the head of one or other of the shaggy collie-dogs, which lay basking on the hearth; and the decorum proper for saying a lesson would be forgotten for a moment, while the dimpled features relaxed into a roguish smile, as if it were very hard to keep up the proper amount of gravity to the end. The blue eyes turned to look at Davie as he entered, but the master made a sign to the new-comer to seat himself at the other side of the fire, and recalled his pupil's wandering attention with these words,—" Not yet, my Bonnie Bell; thou shalt hear all about it afterwards. Go on; we had just come to the first verse of the twenty-third Psalm,—'The Lord is my Shepherd.'" "'The Lord is my Shepherd; therefore can I lack nothing,'" repeated the child's voice; "'He shall feed me in a——' Down, Chevy, lass! Shag, lie down!" " Isabella!" The child looked up, shook her curls back, and went on again:—"'In a green pasture: and lead me forth beside the waters of comfort.'" So she went steadily on, till at the fourth verse she paused.— " Daddy, where's the Valley of the Shadow of Death? Shall I ever go there?" The strong man shuddered and turned pale, a spasm passed over his face, and he closed the book hastily. He had married late in life, his wife was dead, and this, the child of his old age, was as the apple of his eye,—as the one little ewe lamb. " God forbid, my child, don't talk of it. That'll do for to-night; now go to Davie, and hear about Meg."

The child stood for a moment, with her wide blue eyes fixed full upon her father, half puzzled, half meditative; then she nodded her curly head once or twice, whispering to herself,—" Never mind; I'll ask old John Armstrong, some day; *he'll* know;" after which, having apparently made up her mind in a satisfactory manner, she threw all puzzling thoughts to the winds, sprang upon Davie's knee, seated herself there with the air of a little queen, and demanded to hear the promised story. Adventures and tea satisfactorily disposed of, Bonnie Bell left her father and Davie to discuss the sheep, and seated herself among their shaggy guardians. It was a pretty sight, a group worthy of Sir Edwin

Landseer. In the centre was the child's
figure, her curly head resting against a great
rough sheep-dog, which sat bolt upright
behind her; while another (Davie's dog)
crouched at her side, using every effort to
attract her attention : at the present this was
given to Chevy, the prime favourite of her
canine court, who occupied the place of
honour, with her soft head resting in the
little mistress's lap. Chevy was a very
beautiful dog, a perfect specimen of the race,
with a fine, silky coat of warm cinnamon
colour, deepening to rich brown on her ears
and long feathery tail.

It was a very pleasant evening to Davie,
but it came to an end all too soon, for when
the clock struck eight, he prudently took his
leave, not wishing for another chapter of
lamentations from his grandmother. Bonnie
Bell accompanied him to the door, and Davie
turned back several times to wave his hand to
the pretty child, who stood at the half-open
door, letting a long track of warm light shine

out upon the snow, and, even when he was out of sight, he still heard her clear, ringing voice calling after him, — " Good night, Davie !"

CHAPTER IV.

THE SQUIRREL'S FAULT.

Our hero was leaning idly over the garden gate, spending his Sunday evening in watching the movements of the newly-arrived swallows, as they darted about hither and thither, making terrible havoc among the flies and midges, who were enjoying an airy dance in the warm spring sunbeams. Presently old Armstrong came to the cottage door, looked out, and saw his grandson standing in the idle attitude just described. "Davie, lad, aren't ye goin' to church this fine evenin'?" "Well, I dinna ken," replied Davie, hardly troubling to turn round. Old Armstrong looked pained; he hesitated for a moment, irresolute whether to speak out or not, for he

was a gentle, timid old man, and terribly afraid
of finding fault; so he stood there tapping his
stick nervously on the ground, and looking
straight before him, as though he were
wholly taken up with the manœuvres of two
kitty wrens, who were popping in and out of
the hedge, with feathers and bits of moss in
their tiny beaks, evidently intent on building
a nest behind scenes. At last, after a considerable amount of tapping and coughing, the old
man seemed to have made up his mind, and,
without allowing himself a minute in which
to lose courage, burst out abruptly,—" Davie,
lad, ye maun (*must*) e'en go to church; sich
(*such*) like goings on canna be allowed.
Here's Sunday after Sunday brings the same
story; when I ask ye, will ye go? it's aye ' I
dinna ken.' Lad, lad, think better on't.
Ye're hard to guide, and God kens it hurts
me to have to speak to ye; but I must, lad,
I must. I canna let ye go to the bad, as I
sorely fear ye're doin', wi'out sayin' a word
to stop ye. Come, get yer Prayer-book, like

a good lad, and let me see ye go." Davie
stood still a moment without moving; then
he turned round sulkily, went into the house,
got his Prayer-book, and set off, without a
word.

It was a lovely evening, the sun was
getting low, and threw a slanting flood of
warm yellow light over the whole country.
The hills lay peaceful and still behind a soft veil
of hazy blue, which hid all the scars and
wrinkles which time and tempest had marked
so deeply in their rugged sides, and made
them look young and fair, as when God first
created them. Every stream and burn flashed
like molten gold in the evening splendour;
lambs were bleating far up among the hills,
and from the heathy uplands came thrilling
clear the liquid call of the curlew. It was a
scene of holy rest; but I am afraid Davie had
anything but holy thoughts in his heart. In
the first place, he was terribly vexed at being,
as he would have called it, lectured by his
grandfather, for the companions he had been

with of late were used to talk very big about
the "rights of man," and the nonsense of
being under control, and about the propriety
of everybody pleasing themselves, &c.   All
which very wrong and foolish ideas Davie
had, I am sorry to say, taken up much too
readily.   Then he had been to church so
seldom of late, and had, besides, been spending
his time in such questionable society and in
such a very questionable manner, to say the
least of it, that he had a great objection to
putting himself in the Rector's way, lest he
should be taken to task for his shortcomings;
for the latter would, as Davie well knew,
think nothing of stopping him with a sudden.
"Why have you not been at church lately,
my lad?" and Davie felt that he should be
at his wit's end for an answer to that plain,
straightforward question.   So he made no
haste whatever to reach his destination, but
sauntered on leisurely through the green
fields, where the bright blossoms of the pile-
wort were making the grass golden with their

yellow stars, and the cowslips were beginning
to think of hanging out their spotted bells.
And when he came to the gate leading into
Kirkside Wood, he even treated himself to
two or three swings, big boy as he was;
though all the time he could not but hear the
bell pealing up from the valley, and making
the hills ring with its vibrating echoes.
Then, when he had tired of that, there was a
stick to be cut and peeled, and of course when
the latter operation is going on, quick walk-
ing is out of the question. And then the
woods were so beautifully green and still,
with thousands of tiny leaves just bursting
into life, and a host of yellow primroses mus-
tering under every tuft of moss and lifting
up their innocent child-faces from beneath
every fallen tree, as though looking out for a
kiss from their kinsfolk the golden sunbeams,
which peeped down from among the branches,
making such a twinkling chequer-work on
the path, all brown with last year's fir-needles.
Hidden somewhere among the tree-tops, a

cuckoo was making the woods ring with his
sweet spring-notes, to which the wood-pigeons
kept up a soft crooning accompaniment. Who
could hurry through such a scene as this?
Davie, it appeared, could not, or shall I say
would not? perhaps that would be the truer
expression of the two; for we have all wills
of our own, and few things are impossible
when we choose to set *them* to work. At all
events, the bell had ceased ringing before our
hero was half way through the wood, but this
did not seem to disturb him in the least, not
a bit of it, for he did not even quicken his
pace, but strolled on as leisurely as ever,
taking infinite pains not to leave a shred of
peel on the long straight willow-wand which
was rapidly blanching under his knife. So
much attention was he giving to this in-
teresting occupation, that a loud "Hullo,
David!" quite close to him, made him give
such a start, that the greeting was quickly
followed up by a ringing peal of laughter,
and raising his eyes in some confusion, he

encountered a shower of jokes from some half-
dozen lads of his acquaintance, who were re-
clining in all sorts of comfortable attitudes on
the moss round the roots of a great Scotch fir.

"Good e'en to ye, Davie! Hope your reflections were pleasant." "Sorry to spoil such
a jolly dream, Armstrong; but I'd like to
know what it was a' about?" "A penny for
your thoughts, lad. Come, sit down, and let
us have the benefit of them." "I say, Jack,
hold your tongue," said Davie to the last
speaker, a lad of about his own age, and his
favourite companion; "I wasn't thinkin'
about naught, if it wasn't this stick. I say,
isn't it a jolly straight one?" "First-rate,"
returned Jack; "let's see't, lad?" Davie gave
it into his friend's hand. "First-rate," repeated the latter, bending it gingerly with
the air of a connoisseur; "I say, I wouldn't
like a taste o' *this*. But come, lad, sit down,
won't ye? it's jolly comfortable here;" and
Master Jack let himself drop lazily back on
the moss, with his snub nose pointing up to

the sky, and the sunbeams adding new
freckles to the plentiful supply already adorn-
ing his ruddy face. " Well, I dinna think I
can stay wi' ye," said Davie, in reply to this
tempting invitation, " I'm precious late as
it is." " What for? where're ye bound?"
asked another lad. " Where d'ye think,
Dick? where does this road lead to?"
" To the church? Oh, I say, I didna think
ye were sich a precious fool as to be goin'
there, sich a bonnie evenin' as this is."
" Hullo, Davie, I thought ye'd got out o'
leadin'-strings by now!" exclaimed a third.
" I dinna ken what ye mean," replied Davie
quickly, " I——" " Just hold your tongues,"
put in Jack, " Davie 'll stay fast enough if
ye ask him civilly, won't ye, Davie?" " Well,
I dinna ken," began Davie, in a rather
hesitating tone. " Yes, ye do," interrupted
Jack; " come, ye'd better stay at once, lad,
or the lads 'll think it's 'cause you're afraid."
" Oh, ho! that's it, is it!" cried two or three
at once, in a jeering tone, " he's afraid o' the

Rector !" Davie coloured fiery red and answered shortly, " No, I'm not." "Then it's
your grandfather?" Ay, *that's* it !" " No, it
isn't," answered Davie, hotly; and yet I think
both these names gave him a pang. " What
then ?" continued the tempters in the same
tone. " Oh, I ken the poor lile bairn's (*little
child*) afraid o' his grannie ! ha, ha !" " Say
that again, if ye dare !" exclaimed Davie pas-
sionately, " I tell ye I'm afraid o' nobody !"
" Can't ye be quiet, you fellows ?" said Jack
again, with a wink to his comrades, as much
as to say, " *I'll* manage him." "Come, Davie
lad, of course ye're not afraid, but ye'll stay
when *I* ask ye, won't ye? I havena had a crack
(*chat*) wi' ye since I don't know when. Come,
it's no use thinkin' o' church now, it's far too
late ; the bell's given over ringin' this long
while. Come !" He made room· on the grass
beside him, and Davie, either convinced that it
was too late to go on, or afraid of his companions' mockery, let himself be persuaded, and
threw himself on the moss by his friend's side.

"That's right, Armstrong; I like to see a man use his freedom, and not submit to be kept down by anybody. It's showing a proper spirit."

This last speech was made by Tom Barton, a young man some years older than the rest, to whom Davie had been recently introduced by Jack. He had not been long in the place, and no one knew much about him; but he had lived for some time in Newcastle, and gave himself the airs of a town man, for which he was much admired by these simple country lads. He now treated his more ignorant companions to a very grandiloquent discourse on his favourite theme, the rights of man, which was listened to in respectful silence, though most of the boys privately considered it rather dull, and I believe it was a considerable relief to them all when Jack suddenly broke in with an excited—" I say, there's the jolliest squirrel ye ever saw!" and immediately started to his feet, followed by the whole party, with the exception of Tom Barton, who sat still, smiling contempt-

E

uously at the rustics who could prefer such a
small amusement to the rational conversation
with which he had been regaling them.
Poor little squirrel! its pleasant gambols
were quickly interrupted by a perfect cannonade of stones and sticks, which rattled
among the branches, bringing down a return
volley of fir-cones upon the heads of the
besiegers, which, however, did not daunt
them in the least, and the cannonade was
kept up with unabated vigour. The squirrel
sprang from branch to branch and from tree
to tree, followed closely by its persecutors.
Now it seemed lost to sight, and again a
glimpse of its long bushy tail called forth a
shout of triumph, and a loud "There it is,
there it is!" "Send your stones a bit higher,
Davie!" "There, you've hit it, Dick!" "No,
it's away up that tree." "Which?" "Why,
that tall thin larch-tree!" "Oh, I say, if I
don't believe that's its nest! D'ye see? I'll
warrant it's got a brood o' young uns!" The
lads clustered round the foot of the tree,

looking longingly at the dark object in the fork of one of the topmost branches, which they felt certain contained the ardently desired prize. But how was it to be got at? The larch was alarmingly slender and very bare of branches for some way up, and, moreover, it stood uncomfortably overhanging the steep bank, which went sheer down to the lower road by the river-side. It would take a bold climber to attempt that tree. For some moments the boys stood eyeing the nest in silence; then our friend Davie spoke. "I say, all this lookin' 'll not get us the squirrels, and it'd be so jolly to have one to put in a cage." "So it would, lad," returned Jack. "I say, Davie, won't ye try it? Ye're the best climber among us, out and out." "Well, I dinna much care if I do," answered Davie. "Give us a back, lad." And taking off his boots, he mounted on Jack's back, and taking a firm grip, began swarming up the bare trunk. He was an agile climber, and though the tree quivered and shook in a

most disagreeable manner, he soon succeeded
in gaining the lower branches, and once
there, went up like a cat. Now and then a
bough cracked under his foot, and the
anxious gazers held their breath with fright,
but Davie always recovered his balance immediately, and went on as boldly as ever.
As he neared the top, however, it was neces-
sary to be much more careful, for the tree
was now very slender, and swayed and shivered so, that even he had his doubts as to
whether it would be possible to reach the
desired branch in safety. By dint of great
care, however, it was accomplished; the
eager hand was stretched out, and, to the
boy's intense delight, it came in contact
with something soft and warm, and raising
himself cautiously up, his eyes were charmed
by the sight of four tiny squirrels coiled up
on a bed of softest moss and lichen. Eager
were the faces down below, so eager and
attentive to what was going on in the
tree-top, that their owners never thought of

taking any note of the doings below; great, therefore, was their consternation on hearing Tom Barton exclaim, " I say, you lads, you'd better make yourselves scarce, if you don't want a blowing up; here's the woodman, and I don't know who besides, coming along the road; I believe the Rector's there, too, they're likely out of church by this time. Look out !"

He did not need to speak twice, for with never a thought of waiting for their comrade aloft, the lads took to their heels and were quickly out of sight. The squirrels were saved; Davie's hand was hastily withdrawn, and he set about coming down the tree in double-quick time. To get down from his elevated position without being discovered, was now his greatest wish, and he paid little attention to cracking branches and swaying trunk in his hurried descent. It was nearly accomplished, his object was all but attained, when a rotten branch, on which he had unwarily set his foot, suddenly snapped, and

his descent was finished in a manner a great
deal more speedy than he could have wished.
Over and over he rolled down the hill, and
would probably have gone right to the
bottom, had it not been for a forest of
withered ferns and nettles, into which he
tumbled, and which saved him from a broken
leg, and, likely enough, from what would
have been a great deal worse—a broken neck.
As it was, he lay for some time half stunned,
and very much bruised and scratched, and it
was not for several minutes that he could at
all recover his senses, or remember what had
happened. Presently, however, he sat up,
and leaning on one hand, looked towards the
road. No one was there; the people, whoever
they might have been, had passed, and not a
trace remained of his faithless companions.
The best thing, then, was to get up and
make his way home as fast as possible; but
this was not so easily done, for as soon as
Davie tried to walk, he found that he had
twisted his ankle, and the pain was such, that

it was all he could do to crawl up to the top
of the hill, and sit down sick and faint, at the
foot of the tree where the squirrel had been
first seen. Oh, how he wished that there
were no such things as squirrels in the
world! But it was too late to wish any such
thing now, even if the poor innocent little
creatures could have been dispensed with
from their place in creation, on purpose to
save Master Davie from the consequences of
a fault, which would have been none the less
inexcusable if one of their species had never
appeared on the scene as an instrument of
punishment. But Davie never thought of
this; oh, no! it was not *his* fault at all,—it
was all that abominable squirrel; if it had
not been for the little wretch, he should have
been safe at home by this time, and no one
would have been a bit the wiser. So thought
Master Davie; but such reflections not being
at all calculated to help him home, he presently got up again, and picking up a large
stick (not the one he had wasted so much

time in peeling, but a good strong serviceable
staff, in all its native roughness), he began
slowly and painfully to limp home. And a
weary walk it was—very different from what
it had been in coming. The sunshine was all
gone now, the cuckoo was silent, the primroses had shut up their creamy leaves, and as
for poor Davie himself, all his grand spirit of
independence had vanished, and it was hard,
hard work to keep back the tears, as he
dragged himself along, leaning heavily on
his stick, his ankle so terribly painful, that
he had to stop and rest many times, hardly
knowing how he should bear to go on again.
This being the case, it was quite dark when
at length he reached home, and opening the
door, staggered in, and dropped into a seat.
Old Armstrong and his wife looked in
astonishment at their grandson, not knowing
what had come over him. "Why, Davie lad,
what ails ye?" exclaimed the old man, rising
from his seat and hobbling towards him, as
well as his rheumatic joints would allow him;

"what is it, laddie?" he added tenderly, bending over the boy. "Hinnies me, he's going off into a faint!" cried the old grandmother, alarmed by the boy's deadly paleness, and rushing off for a glass of water. But it was not quite so bad as that. The rest and the cold water soon restored Davie, and, relieved from her alarm, his grandmother began a torrent of questions, to which Davie, I am sorry to say, gave her very short answers. "But what ails ye, lad? If ye winna say how ye came by the mishap, ye might at least tell a body what it is." "It's my ankle, of course," replied Davie crossly, "I gave't a bit twist, like." "Aye, aye, it's always the way; ye're always gettin' into some mischief or other. Let's see, and I'll bathe your foot." She suited the action to the word, and Davie was glad to let her do it, for though he could not help wincing during the getting off of the boot and stocking, the warm water was very soothing to the swollen ankle. "But how did ye come by it, Davie?"

asked his grandfather, when the bathing was
over, and the foot tied up in a cold-water
bandage, " ye've surely been playing yourself,
instead of going to. church." Davie looked
into the fire and sat silent; in spite of his
many faults, there was something in the lad
which would not let him tell a lie. Old
Armstrong did not press the point; he also
sat silent for some time, and a very sad
expression came over his gentle old face;
then, almost as if he were thinking aloud, he
murmured,—"He winna heed me, I canna
make him keep straight. What would his
father do, if he kent (*knew*) how his bairn
was goin' on? Puir Geordie! he was aye a
good lad, it was hard to lose him sae (*so*)
early, and his bonnie bit wife too! But
no, God kens best;. it would maybe have
broken their hearts to see the only bairn they
had, goin' clean contrary to what's right.
Aye, aye, God help us!" And still Davie
did not speak; if he *were* touched, he would
not show it. The lads who were now his

constant companions had put it into his head that his grandparents wanted to keep him in leading-strings, and this touched his pride, and made him harden his heart against anything they might say, being determined to prove that he was a man, and would have his own will. Foolish lad! he had yet to learn that true manliness consists, not in yielding to temptation from fear of ridicule, but in resisting it boldly, firmly, and keeping steadily on in the right path, because it *is* right, careless as to what others may say or do. The sprained ankle kept him out of mischief for a week or so, but when that was healed, I am afraid he forgot all about this little lesson, as you will presently see.

CHAPTER V.

"SHEW-w-w! How away! How away! Hie Laddie! set them round. Whew-w-w!" So shouted our friend Davie, as he drove his flock of unruly black-faced mountain sheep along the road, on the last Thursday in May, to be sold at the Alston Fair. The morning was fine, and the many passers-by sadly frightened the poor sheep, fresh from the quiet fells. Now a spring-cart rattled by, filled with fair-bound lasses, their gay bonnets covered with clean white handkerchiefs tied under the chin, as a protection against positive dust and possible rain. Now a jolly farmer trotted ponderously past, mounted on his heavy cart-horse, with his buxom wife behind him. Then, perhaps, a saucy gig would dash right through the

flock, scattering the sheep right and left,
while Davie bawled at them till he was red
in the face, and Laddie rushed from side to
side, barking energetically, now turning the
frightened creatures, as they tried to bolt
into a field; now seizing a runaway by the
wool, and dragging it back to the rest by
main force. The country was looking lovely.
Long lines of fleecy morning-mist marked
the winding course of the river, and changed
to rainbow colours, as the warm May sunbeams full upon them. The light breeze
blew whole fleets of tiny white cloudlets
across the bright blue sky, causing a glorious
play of light and shadow on the violet hills
below, each effect seeming more wondrously
beautiful than the last. Where the road
wound through the coppice-wood, there was
the loveliest little "bit," as artists say, that
one could wish to see. To the right, the
wood descended precipitously to the shining
river; to the left, it rose as steeply, in tier
above tier of graceful larches, feathered down

to the tips of their slender branches, with a
veil of vivid greenery, through which shone
the carmine rosettes of fir-cones yet to be.
Velvety moss, in all conceivable shades of
green and gold, tapestried the rough stone
walls on either side of the road, over which
stretched the gnarled branches of the haw-
thorns, white with perfumy " summer snow ;"
while through the sombre green of the spruces
and Scotch firs, one could catch lovely little
glimpses of a purple background of hills,
with Cross Fell, still wearing his white cap,
towering above them, and the little town of
Alston, which boasts ·of being the highest
market-town in England, nestling at their feet.

The little town, usually so quiet and sleepy,
was all astir this morning with holiday folk ;
grey-plaided shepherds and herdsmen drove
their horned sheep, and hornless, shaggy
black cattle up the steep narrow street,
leading to the Fair Hill, shouting and hal-
looing at the top of their voices.   Stalwart
mountaineers, with their dogs at their heels,

pressed through the crowd, elbowing their
fellows good-humouredly right and left, as
they took their way to the grand scene of
buying and selling. The market-place was
thronged with people intent on business or
pleasure. Women with their baskets on
their arms, sat on the dilapidated steps of
the old market cross, which, by-the-by, is not
a cross at all, but a very tumble-down roof,
supported on eight time-worn pillars, and
surmounted by a gas-lamp. On all sides
were erected temporary stalls, loaded with
wooden dairy-utensils, oranges and apples,
gingerbread horses of a peculiar species
unknown to naturalists, sticks of toffy,
gorgeously painted sugar-candy, and non-
descript goods of every sort. Here some
men were putting up a wooden peep-show,
there a Cheap Jack was perched in front of
his travelling-waggon, filling the air with
cries of, " Who'll buy? who'll buy? who'll
buy? The most beautiful mirror ever made,
fit to reflect your bonnie faces, my winsome

lasses ! dirt cheap ; come, who'll buy ? Have
a fine pocket-knife, my lad ? Sheffield-made,
I'll warrant ye, on my honour ! Never was a
sharper blade. Come, it's going for a mere
song ; who'll buy ?" &c.   It was a bright,
pretty scene, all sunshine and merriment,
that the irregular, steep-gabled old houses
round the market-place looked down upon ;
and many was the hearty laugh, and rough
country joke, that echoed from their white-
washed walls, as the gaily dressed fair-folk
poured in from every side.

Davie had much ado to pioneer his flock
through the throng, and he certainly would
never have succeeded in doing so at all, had
it not been for the able assistance of Laddie,
who kept his charge together in famous
style, like a wise dog as he was.   In the
potato-market, Davie encountered his master,
coming down the hill with rapid strides ;
he stopped to tell our hero that, being called
away on business, he would probably not be
able to return to the town that day, and so

F

must leave the entire charge of selling the
sheep in Davie's hands. "Do your best to
make a good bargain, my lad," he said, as
he walked off, "and mind, don't stop late, or
get to bad work with any 'o' the idle fellows."
Davie did not much relish this last injunction,
and it was with rather an affronted feeling
that he drove his flock on to the Fair Hill,
and stood there waiting for a bidder. It was
some time before one appeared, and longer
still before our hero was able to come to
terms with anybody; but at last the bargain was struck, and the whole of the sheep
disposed of to a respectable farmer, well
known to Davie and his master. "There,"
he said, taking three sovereigns out of a
little canvas bag, and handing them to the
young shepherd, "take these now, and ye
shall have the rest to-morrow. I bought as
bonnie a cow as ye ever saw, just now; and
she cost a little more than I thought to
spend; but your master 'll trust me. Don't
lose the siller, there's a cannie lad!" "Not

I," replied Davie, thinking the farmer might have spared his advice; and putting the money into a little bag which served him as a purse, he tied a string round the neck, and put it in his pocket. Just as he turned to go, he espied Tom Barton at his elbow, watching with great interest a horse which was being put through its paces in the ring; he gave our hero a condescending nod, which was returned by the latter as he walked away, with Laddie at his heels, to take his share in the amusements which were going forward.

A day of merry-making passes quickly, and by the time Davie had enjoyed half a dozen rides in a round-about, had taken a leisurely stroll through the town from end to end, had invested sixpence of his half-crown in one of the vaunted Sheffield knives, and another threepence in sugar-candy for Bonnie Bell, the Town Hall clock chiming seven, warned him that it was time to go. He whistled to Laddie, and was in the act of

leaving the market-place, when some one
touched him on the shoulder, and turning
round, whom should he see but Jack Robson.
"I say, lad, where are ye off to?" was his
greeting. "Home," replied Davie; "it's gettin' late, and I've master's sheep to see to."
"Oh, can't ye stop a bit longer? There's a
wild-beast show just come into town, and
it'll be open in half an hour. I hear tell
there's the stunningest elephant you ever
saw, and a performing bear, and I don't know
what all!" "Oh, I *say!*" responded Davie,
"an' I never saw any wild beasts before;
I'd like well to stay. How long will't be
afore it's opened, d'ye say?" "Only half
an hour," replied Jack quickly. "Ye'd tied
(*might as well*) stop, lad." "I'd like well,"
repeated Davie longingly. "Oh, I say! I'll
let the sheep be, to-night, for once in a way;
it isn't often one has the chance o' seein'
wild beasts." "That's right, lad!" replied
Jack; "let's away up by the caravan, the
lions are roarin' awful."

The menagerie had taken up its position before one of the numerous inns, whose sign-boards make Alston a perfect gallery of native art. A crowd was gathered round the lumbering waggon, waiting impatiently for the opening of the show, and listening with awe-struck countenances to the ominous roars, and savage, outlandish noises, which from time to time issued from the interior. As might have been expected, the show was not ready at the appointed time, and it was much nearer eight than half-past seven, when the showman at length threw open the doors, and began to exhibit his wonders. They were not much to boast of, and Davie was rather disappointed in his expectations; the elephant seemed to him to be very small, the lions were miserable, broken-spirited creatures, very different from his idea of what the king of beasts should be ; and the bears performed nothing more wonderful than a rough attempt at a dance on their hind legs. It was a sorry affair, and Davie could not help feel-

ing that he had gained very little pleasure
by his sacrifice of duty. Still, after the show
was over, he lingered about the inn-door,
laughing and joking with the idle lads assem-
bled there, regardless alike of his master's in-
junctions and of the late hour, regardless, too,
of that prayer which he had once been taught
but so little heeded now,—"Lead us not into
temptation." Nine o'clock chimed from the
tower of the Town Hall; a cold drizzling
rain came on, and Davie began to turn longing glances towards the warm fire-light
which streamed from the inn-door, every
time it opened to admit a customer. Jack saw
the direction of his friend's eyes and said,
—"Let's go in, Davie lad, and have a drop
o' somethin' warm; it's comin' on cold, to-
night." Davie hesitated; to his credit be it
said, he had never sat down to any sort of
drink in a public-house before, and he shrank
from doing so now. "Oh, I say, I can't!
It's awfully late, and I really must be off."
"Nonsense, lad," said the voice of Tom

Barton behind him. "You'll have a long
walk in the wet, and it's ill settin' off without a drop to warm you; come, don't be a
fool." "Yes, Davie, ye'll do't to please me,
won't ye?" urged Jack, "it's so unsociable to
refuse to sit down wi' a friend, when one asks
ye, and it's only once in a way, after all."

Davie thought there really was some truth
in this, and he yielded, thinking he would
just take one glass to satisfy them, and then
be off. Foolish lad! he little thought what
he was bringing on himself. "I say, Davie,"
whispered Jack, as they entered the public-
house, "I haven't got any tin, have ye?"
"To be sure," answered our hero, taking out
the remains of his half-crown, "I'll treat ye,
Jack." He ordered some whiskey, and the
three lads joined a noisy group, who were
sitting round the fire, drinking and laughing
and singing uproariously. Davie's conscience
pricked him at first, and he felt awkward in
the unaccustomed situation in which he found
himself; but the merriment was infectious,

and a few jokes from Tom Barton, about a "fledgling" and a "milksop," put him on his mettle, making him wishful to appear as much of a "man" as the rest, and soon he was as merry as any of them. When ten o'clock struck, he jumped up, saying he "really must go now;" but every one exclaimed, one or two laughed jeeringly at his hurry to be home, and, on Tom offering to stand treat this time, the foolish lad suffered himself to be persuaded once more; he had yielded the first time, and the second was easy work. Half-past ten struck, a quarter to eleven, and still he sat on, and when at length he did break away from that evil company, for the first time in his life, Davie was not himself. He had just sense enough left to get home, and to avoid bringing his grandmother's reproaches upon himself by knocking at the house door; he turned into the stable, and throwing himself on a heap of hay, fell into a heavy slumber.

CHAPTER VI.

SIN BRINGS SORROW.

WHEN Davie awoke next morning, the bright sun was shining full in his face; he started up and rubbed his eyes, wondering much how he came to be lying in the stable with his clothes on, and why his head ached so. All too soon, however, the remembrance of last night came back to the poor lad's mind, and, alone as he was, the hot blood rushed to his face at the consciousness of the dreadful disgrace which he had brought upon himself; and, as he thought of all that had happened, his horror at himself became so great, that, sitting down in the darkest corner of the stable, he hid his burning face in his hands in an agony of shame, feeling as though he could never bear to look at anybody again. Presently, however, the necessity of going to his master with the money came into his mind, and wondering how he should manage to get it done, he put his hand into his pocket to feel for the little bag of sovereigns, and— oh, horror, it was gone! This new misfortune seemed almost too dreadful to be believed; with trembling hands, Davie felt in every pocket he possessed, then turned them all inside out and shook them,—in vain, the bag of sovereigns was nowhere to be found!

Poor Davie! if you had seen his horror and despair, you would have pitied him, though it is true he had brought all this sorrow upon himself by his own bad conduct. All that day he wandered about, not daring to tell his master of what had happened, and when towards evening Thomas Reed appeared, coming through the fields towards the cottage, the poor lad felt that he would do anything to avoid meeting him; but this was not to be. "Davie! Davie!" called his master; and sorely against his will, Davie obeyed the summons. Thomas Reed was a kind man on all ordinary occasions; but when sinned against, he was inexorably stern, and breach of trust and intemperance were sins he never forgave. Davie, then, had cause to tremble as he stood before him and saw the iron look on his usually so genial countenance.

"David Armstrong," said the master, in a stern voice, "what is this I hear of your behaviour at the fair, yesterday? Nay, no excuses; I have heard from more than one of the state in which you came home last night, and your own face tells me it is true. Nay, not a word!" (as the boy murmured something in a broken voice,) "I know enough already. Give me my money." "Oh, sir, sir!" said poor Davie, "I haven't got it; somebody must have picked my pocket at the fair." Reed's face grew very dark. "And if they have, whose fault is it? Tell me that." "Mine, I suppose, sir. Oh, sir, I'm very sorry!" "Perhaps you are; but that won't give me

back my money; you should have thought of
that sooner, my fine fellow. I trusted you,
David Armstrong, and this is how you repay
me. You may look out for another situation,
for I can no longer keep you in my service."

At these words Davie grew white with
dismay, and the tears rose to his eyes. "Oh,
sir!" he cried brokenly, "won't you forgive
me this once? It's the first time, and I'll
never do't again!" But Reed had already
walked away, with his heart steeled against
the poor lad's entreaties. It was hard measure,
a bitter punishment for a first offence: justice
without mercy is what we could not bear from
God, and what are we that we mete it to our
fellow-men? We should be very careful how
we do so, for has He not said,—"With what
measure ye mete, it shall be measured to you
again?" Poor Davie! it was a grievous time
for him, and bitterly he repented the sin
which had brought such sorrow upon him.
They had to leave the dear little home on the
hill-side, to make room for the new shepherd,

and go to one much smaller and meaner on the other side of the Fell : this was hard for Davie, but he found his grandmother's ceaseless lamentations and reproaches, and his grandfather's silent sorrow, harder still to bear.

One Sunday afternoon, unable longer to endure the plaints of the former, he wandered down towards the little church. It was a hot June afternoon, the whole country seemed slumbering in the golden sunlight, which shone with all the sultry glow of midsummer. Down the bracken-covered hill walked Davie with slow steps and a heavy heart, scarcely even seeing the delicate tints of colour on the hazy hills, or the flashing glint of the river, which wound like a blue ribbon round the green meadows, in whose midst stood the little parish church of Kirkhaugh, its white walls gleaming in the sunlight. The service-bell had stopped before Davie reached the little building, and when he got there he did not go in, but stood leaning against the half-open door, listening to the voices within,

longing, yet not daring to enter, for it was
now many months since Davie had been to
church, the consciousness of his wrong-doing
making him afraid to meet his clergyman,
who, however, had sought him at his own
home many times, but always in vain, for the
boy systematically avoided him. Davie did
not stand there long,—he was too much afraid
of being discovered, but wandered slowly up
the hill again, and sitting down under the
shelter of Kirkside Wood, began to cut the
stems of the bracken with his pocket-knife,
in search of the oak-tree mark in the pith,
which may be found by cutting the stalk
across close to the root. Soon, however, he
tired of this, and lying down among the fern,
he pulled his cap over his eyes and went half
asleep. He was aroused by hearing his own
name in a child's sweet voice, and starting up
he saw Bonnie Bell sitting on the grass
beside him. It was the first time he had seen
her, except from a distance, since his disgrace,
and the hot blood mounted to his face before

that little child. " Davie," she said, stroking his hand, " poor Davie, I'm so sorry !"

The blinding tears rushed to the lad's eyes at these simple words of sympathy, the first he had heard for so long, and he turned his face hastily away. "Davie," went on the child, "you're not angry with me, are you? I *have* asked daddy to take you back, and it isna my fault that I didna come to see ye; he wouldna let me." "Oh, Bonnie Bell, my wee pet!" sobbed poor Davie, trying in vain to hide his tears, "dinna speak sae! It's a' my fault; I'm a bad lad, and I dinna ken how I'm ever to be better!" "Oh yes, Davie, ye'll try, won't ye? If ye'd been at church this afternoon, ye'd have heard how to do't. It was *such* a bonnie story, about a shepherd-lad called David, like you; and d'ye ken, one day when he was keepin' his sheep all alone, there came a lion and a bear, and took away a wee lamb out of the flock, but David went after them, and killed both the great wild beasts, though they were sae fierce, for God helped him.

And anither time he killed a terrible giant
wi' naught but a stane out o' the burn. And
d'ye ken, Davie, the Rector told us that the
lion and the bear are like our smaller temptations, and the giant like a great one, and if
we resist the wee ones in His name, He will
deliver us from the great ones, just the same;
but then it must be in His name, like David
did; for if we only try by ourselves without
askin' God to help us, we shallna be able
to overcome our temptations, any more than
David could have done, if it hadna been for
Him. I think that was what the Rector said,
Davie; I tried all I could to mind it, for I
liked about it so much. Dear Davie, won't
you try, like that other David did?" The
child put her soft arms round the lad's neck,
as she repeated endearingly, "Won't you try,
Davie?" And David thought he would try,
for wee Bonnie Bell's sake, and went home
feeling happier than he had done for many a
day.

Ah, Davie, take care! Do not be too self-

G

confident; remember that there is One higher than wee Bonnie Bell, for whose sake you must resist temptation, without whom we can do nothing, for with His own blessed lips He has taught us to pray,—" Deliver us from evil."

CHAPTER VII.

THE VOICE OF THE TEMPTER.

THE splendour of an August sunset was resting like a glory over the bonnie hill country. The sky seemed on fire with tongues of rosy flame, which reflected themselves in broken light on the crest of every little wavelet dancing before the breeze, on the clear brown surface of Coanwood Lough, a lone mountain tarn far up among the moors. Half hidden in the wilderness of purple heather, which stretched down to the very brink of the tarn, lay our friend Davie, in an attitude of listless despair. Poor lad, he had much to sadden him; poverty had come to his once comfortable home, for he had been unable to obtain another situation, and the

chance employment which he fell in with
from time to time, went a very little way
towards keeping his old grandparents.   One
by one the few valuables which old Armstrong
possessed had been sold,—his silver watch,
his wife's wedding tea-spoons, the black cow,—
and now Meg was to go, if Davie could not
succeed in earning a little money before the
week's end.   Poor Davie! it wrung his heart
to think of parting with his pony,—she who
had been so useful to him in his work; he
could scarcely bear to look at her, and to
think how soon it must be for the last time.

Thinking of these things, he did not hear a
step coming over the heather, and started to
hear a voice close to him saying,—"I say,
Davie, d'ye ken how many grouse are a brace?"
"No," said Davie, jumping up and catching
sight of Jack, "why?"   "Oh, I only thought
ye might have a mind to earn a little money,
I ken ye're hard up."   "Ye're right there, lad,"
answered Davie, sorrowfully, "Meg's to go
next, if I canna get somethin' afore the week's

end. But what have grouse to do wi' it?"
Jack nodded his head mysteriously. "Well,
lad," he said, "ye mustn't let on about it, but
I've a bit o' a plan I want ye to join in. Ye
say ye dinna ken how much grouse are a
brace? Well, I'll tell ye. There's a chap in
Alston is giving five-and-sixpence to anyone
who brings them, and he asks no questions.
Now I'll tell ye what, one or two lads are
going wi' me on to the moors to-morrow
night to net grouse; will ye join us? There're
seldom night-watchers on, where we're going."
"I say, Jack, what d'ye take me for?" answered
Davie indignantly; "I'm not a poacher!"
" Well," returned Jack, a little disconcerted,
"where's the harm? Lots of fellows do it;
the birds are wild, and I don't see but we've
as much right to them as the gentlefolks.
But of course it's just as you like; ye'll only
have to lose Meg, if ye don't join us, that's
all."

This last suggestion took effect. Instead
of going out of the way of temptation, as he

should have done, Davie stayed to parley.
"And what came of it, last time I went
along wi' ye, Jack?" he said; "I made a fool
o' mysel', and lost three sovereigns, and my
place into the bargain." "Well, ye don't
mean to say ye think *I* stole your money, do
ye? Not but what I could knock the right
nail on the head, if I chose, though," he
added, in a mysterious tone. "Well, who
was't?" asked Davie, eagerly. "I say, Jack,
tell me, there's a good lad." "Oh, aye, I'm
a good lad and everything else *now*, when ye
want to know something; a minute ago I
was a poacher and I don't know what all!
Very nice, Master Davie; but there're two
sides to a penny, ye ken. You won't have
anything to say to *me*, when I ask your help
in a simple matter; and why should I have
anything to say to *you?* eh, lad?" "I say,
Jack, you'd tied (*might as well*) tell me,"
returned Davie, coaxingly, "I never just said
I wouldna gang wi' ye; a fellow canna gang
in for a thing like that, wi'out havin' time to

consider on't, ye ken." "Well," said Jack,
"if you'll promise to think about it, I don't
mind tellin' ye, but ye'll let me know by
to-morrow mornin'?" "All right!" cried
Davie, quickly; "fire away, man!" "Well,
then, I'm certain it was that Tom Barton,
you remember him?" Davie nodded, he
remembered him *too* well. "Well, he left
t'public soon after ye did, that night, and
I followed him to t'door, and saw him take a
bag o' his pocket, and count the money in't;
there were just three sovereigns, and the bag
was yours, as sure as my name's Jack. Ye
needn't doubt me, I was as sober as if I'd had
naught but spring water; I'm not such
a fledgling as ye, Davie, and a glass or two
doesna hurt me. And more—forbye what
I saw wi' my own eyes—Tom disappeared
out of the country next day, takin' two
shillin' o' mine, I lent him some time ago,
and which I never expect to set eyes on
again, no more that ye will your three
sovereigns, Davie, for the police have been

after him for other robberies, and they say he's off to America. Now, what d'ye say, lad?" Davie had nothing to say, for the story only served to confirm certain suspicions of his own.

You will wonder that, with this lesson before his eyes, he did not at once refuse to join in Jack's plan; but no, he had let the wily fellow draw him into a kind of bargain, and though he had by no means made up his mind to take part in the poaching expedition, he did not like to offend his comrade, and went away promising to "think about it." *To think about it!* Aye, that is just the mischief. Temptation, to be overcome, must be resisted on the spot; once admit an unworthy thought into the mind, and there is no knowing how soon it may bring forth fruit. "Resist the devil, and he will flee from you," is the advice of the holy Apostle; begin to parley with him, as Eve did with the serpent, and what surety have we that we shall not fall, as she did? But the Tempter had a harder struggle with Davie this time, for lately the lad had really been trying to be better; the fault lay in his having neglected to ask God's help, and striving in his own strength he failed. Poor Meg herself innocently put the finishing stroke to his defeat by running to him, as he was descending the hill-side, whinnying, and putting her nose into his hand. Davie stroked her bonnie head, and the tears came into his eyes at the thought of parting with her. "No, I canna do it," he said, half aloud. "Oh, Meg, my wee lass, you shan't be sold. Poaching really isn't much harm, after a', and I *must* have the money; I *can't* part wi' my pony!" Next morning he sought out Jack, and appointed to meet him on the moors the following evening.

CHAPTER VIII.

OLD ARMSTRONG'S WATCH.

" WHERE's the lad off too?" said old Armstrong to his wife, as he lighted his pipe and sat down by the fire for a smoke, before going to bed. " Off to? Dear knows!" returned Mrs. Armstrong querulously, from her station at the table where she was washing up the supper-things; "it's always the way now-a-days; I wonder ye allow it, John, I do. The lad 'll be doin' somethin' to bring the law upon him, one of these fine days, if things go on in this way. It wasn't the way when *I* was a lass. Father kept the lads wi' a tight hand, he did. I'd like to have seen any goings out o' nights at Burnfoot, I would! But ye were aye too easy, John, ye

were that!" and Mrs. Armstrong rattled the
mugs in the bowl, and used her towel with
extraordinary energy. Old Armstrong sighed
heavily. "Well, Nancy, ye may be right;
maybe I've not been sae strict wi' the lad as
I ought to hae been. But then he was puir
Geordie's only one, ye ken, and it went hard
wi' me to cross him. And he was always
sich a fine-tempered little chap when he was
a bairn! Eh dear, why will lads grow up?
they're none so easy to guide then! There
was Geordie, to be sure, *he* never gave me
any trouble from the hour he was born to
that awfu' day when they brought him in
dead—killed a' of a moment i' the mine-
blastin'; but then there's not many lads like
him. Nancy, lass, ye maunna (*must not*) be
hard on the laddie for his father's sake."
"Aye, John, that's just like ye now, castin'
up things against me!" exclaimed Mrs. Armstrong, in her most lamentable tone, using
her towel vigorously, not to the cups but to
her own eyes; "ye ken well enough I felt

puir Geordie's death as sorely as ever ye did,
and yet ye go for to say that I'm like to be
hard on his bairn! I take it vara (*very*)
unkind o' ye John, I do. If *I*'d had the
guidin' o' the lad, he'd not have been vexin'
us as he is now. It's ye as have ruined him,
John, it is!" "Well, well, wife, dinna let us
have words about it," returned old Armstrong; "ye ken weel I meant to throw
nae blame on ye. The Lord forgie me if
I've failed i' my duty towards the lad, and
may He help him to return to the right
way!"

The old man bowed his head reverently,
and sat looking fixedly into the fire, while his
wife bustled about the room, putting everything tidy for the night. When all was in
order, she went to the window, and stood
looking out. It was nearly dark, large drops
of rain were pattering against the glass, and
the wind had risen, and was sighing drearily
in the old fir-trees outside. "It's comin' in a
wet night," she said, returning towards the

fire; "I was afraid on't when t'sun went down
sae fiery-like. I wish the lad was in!" And
then she stood silent, looking into the fire.
Presently, however, she moved. "Aren't ye
comin' to bed, John? It's nae use waitin'
up any longer." But the old man had taken
down the Bible, and sat reading it with the
aid of his spectacles; he started and looked
up at his wife's voice. "Aye, you go to bed,
Nancy, I maun bide up. There's Lee o' the
Hills, he's given our Davie charge o' a few
sheep he has feedin' up here; he sets par-
tic'ler store by them, and wants them driven
in, whenever it's like to be stormy. If the
lad doesna come in soon, I must e'en go and
look after them mysel'." "*Ye* go, John!
Why, hinnies me, ye're clean dement (*out of
your senses*) to think o' sich a thing, sae bad
as ye are wi' the rheumatics, whenever ye get
the least cold. Why, man, it's enough to gie
ye your death!" "It canna be helped, Nancy.
If the sheep are neglected it'll cost the lad
dear, and though it's not like reg'lar work,

being only for a while, like, yet no one'll trust
, him again, and he finds it hard enough to get
work, poor lad, since he lost Reed's place."
"Aye, and whose fault was that?" asked the
old woman impatiently; "John, ye're gone
clean daft (*quite foolish*) about the lad. But
it's little use me speakin', so I may just as
weel go to bed."

So saying, she took up her candle and retired into the inner room, leaving her husband
to his weary watch. All was very quiet when
she was gone. The rain pattered against the
window, and the wind moaned in the fir-trees,
but these natural night-voices only made the
silence more felt within the room, the peat-
fire burned noiselessly, and the old clock
ticked off the passing moments with a slow
warning voice; then there would come a
rustle among the leaves of the Bible, as the
old man slowly turned them over; but that
was all,—not a step nor a sound to tell of the
returning truant. Stretched before the fire
lay Davie's dog, slumbering profoundly, his

ears now and then twitching lightly, as something in his canine dreams acted on the muscles. The old man looked at him and sighed as he returned to his book, for well he knew that Laddie would be awake in a moment to the slightest sign of his master's return.

So the time went on for an hour or so; then old Armstrong rose, laid away the Bible, and opening the door, stood on the threshold looking out. There was a moon in the sky, but great ragged clouds kept scudding before it, intercepting the light in such a manner that only now and then a wild sudden flood would stream over the country, showing the black massive forms of the hills, and gleaming fitfully in the pools of water made by the rain, which still fell from time to time in flying scuds before the wind. Old Armstrong stood there for some moments looking out, then Laddie got up, stretched his long shaggy legs, and came to look out too. "Well, he's not comin'," said the old man half aloud, as he

closed the door; "there's nothing for't,
Laddie, but to go and do his work for him.
Eh, dear, dear!" He sighed, stooped to pat
the dog, who was leaping up, delighted at
the prospect of going out, and then·muffled
himself in his plaid, set his old Scotch bonnet
on his thin grey locks, lighted a lantern,
and sallied forth, leaning on his staff. "Come,
Laddie, good dog," he said, "come, ye'll help
me fine, won't ye? The sheep winna be far
off, they aye keep down about the house
where the grass is best. Eh, but I wish the
lad wad' tak' tent (*take heed*) to his ways!"

So saying, the old man moved slowly on,
across the little plot of ground which had
once been a garden (but having no one to tend
it, had now become an untidy wilderness of
weeds), through the broken gate·in the tum-
bledown stone wall, and so on to the open hill-
side. Stumbling many a time, splashing into
unseen pools of water, but ever going on,
though with painful steps and feeble trembling
limbs, all for the love he bore to the fatherless

boy of his only son. Poor old man! It seemed
hard that such gentle loving-kindness should
be lavished on one who made it such a poor
return. As for Laddie, he seemed determined
to show that, however much his young master
might neglect his duty, *he* would not follow
his example, for he appeared bent on doing
the work of both. You should have seen
how he bounded on, obedient to the least
sign from his feeble companion; rushing
about, barking energetically, finding the
scattered sheep in the darkness, and finally
driving them all down-hill, with a trium-
phant bark, as much as to say,—"Here they
are, all's right now!"

Old Armstrong drew a deep breath of
relief, as the little flock rushed past him
helter-skelter, their long white fleeces just
visible in the light of a passing moon-gleam.
"The Lord be thanked," he murmured, "the
poor lad's saved from that scrape, at all
events;" and he followed Laddie and his
charge down the hill with a quicker step.

H

The cottage was reached. Though wet and
cold, the old man did not stop till the sheep
were safely housed and foddered, and then
he turned shivering towards the door. He
opened it, and there stood Davie before the
fire, his wet clothes smoking in the glow.
As the door opened, he looked up, his eyes
wide with astonishment. " *Grandfather !*" he
exclaimed. The old man hardly noticed him ;
with his wife's words fresh in his memory,
he kept back the kindly word that rose to
his lips, and forced himself to show dis-
approbation. But it was almost beyond his
strength. Worn out and shivering he came
towards the fire, sank down in his old arm-
chair, and spread his hands towards the
warmth. Davie stood a moment looking at him,
and then turned away pettishly, angry at not
being spoken to. " There'll be them sheep to
be got in next, I suppose," he said. " Come,
Laddie !" But Laddie seeming to understand
quite well, only looked at him and wagged
his tail. " Come along, can't ye ?" continued

the lad impatiently, giving the dog a shove
with his foot. "Let the poor beast alone,
David," said Armstrong, gravely, "he's done
his duty better than you. The sheep are in."
Davie turned round in amazement. "Who
put them in? Grandfather, it's never been
you?" Old Armstrong bowed his head as he
answered, still in the same cold tone, "And
who else was there to do't, David, when you
were away Guid kens where? It's not always
ye'll find anyone to take the duties ye choose
to leave. Don't let it happen again, mind
that, David."

The lad stood for a moment motionless,
his eyes bent on the ground, and a lump
rising in his throat. He was touched to
the quick; one word of his grandfather's
usual gentle kindness would have opened
the whole sealed fountain of the boy's heart,
and he and his grandfather would have
understood each other at last. But that
word did not come. Old Armstrong's was
one of those well-meaning natures, good,

gentle, kindly, but utterly wanting in tact;
lenient when he should have been stern, and
perhaps, as was now the case, suddenly
becoming alive to his former mistakes, and
showing undue severity, when grave kindness
would have had a far better effect. Well,
poor old man, we must not blame him, for
he was forcing himself to do what he thought
was right, and it went sorely against his
gentle heart to have to show coldness to the
child of his dead son. And as for Davie,
knowing as we do what had taken him out
that evening, I do not think we can look on
him as suffering more than he deserved.
" Thank you, grandfather," he said presently;
but the words did not sound like the natural
outpouring of gratitude. Perhaps the old
man was hurt; at all events, he did not make
any response, but sat still and shivered.

It was not for some moments that he
spoke again, and then it was to ask Davie to
help him off with his wet clothes. " I dinna
feel just very well," he said plaintively, " the

cold has stricken me, I fear." Davie obeyed,
but it was with an uneasy conscience and a
heavy heart, and when the old man was gone
to bed, he sat down, leaned his arms upon
the table, dropped his head upon them, and,
big boy though he was, cried bitterly. Poor
Davie! he was very unhappy, and much
cause he had to be so. His attempts on the
game had proved unsuccessful, for the poachers
had been disturbed, and had narrowly escaped
being taken by the keepers. Then he was
angry with himself for going, angry with his
comrade for persuading him, remorseful for
having caused his grandfather to go out on
such a night, and frightened and uncomfortable about the consequences. His fears
proved only too well founded. Poor old
Armstrong was laid up with a worse attack
of rheumatism than he had had for long, and
Davie had to bear the sight of his grandfather's suffering, feeling all the time that he
was the cause of it.

Oh, why will we not pause to think before

doing wrong, of all the misery it is almost certain to entail—misery to ourselves and others? And in this case it happened as it so often does; the evil which was committed that good might come, failed of its end, and poor Meg had to be sold, after all.

CHAPTER IX.

"WHY aren't you supping your soup, my Bonnie Bell?" asked Thomas Reed, one cold winter's day, as he sat at dinner with his little daughter and his old housekeeper in the warm farm-kitchen. The child looked up from her basin of steaming broth, shook back her golden hair, and said coaxingly, "I don't want to sup't, daddy, I want it for somethin' else, and you've not to ask me what. It's a great secret, daddy, a very big secret. There!—I winna say a word more, so its nae use askin' me." She pursed up her wee cherry lips, smiled roguishly, and began feeding herself and Chevy by turns, with bread and cheese. The father laughed at

the show of pretty childish mystery. "Well,
well, my little lass shall keep her secret, and
daddy won't ask her till she tells him. I
have a guess at it, though, ye close little
wench! It's either for a dolls' dinner-party
or else to feed some half-starved cur-dog or
other. Don't do't too often, though, my
canty queen, or I'll be eaten out of house and
home by the brutes; they don't forget the
hand that feeds them, the greedy tykes!"
"Now, dad, that's not fair! you're trying to
find it out, you are! I won't let you say another word!" She jumped up, and put her
dimpled hand before his mouth. Reed shook
it off, laughing; took the little maid in his
arms, and kissed her again and again. She
pretended to struggle. "Daddy, ye scrub me
wi' your grit rough beard." "Hear her, the
minx! Say that again, if ye dare!" He
kissed the little rosy face once more, held
her a moment closely to him, and then put
her down, and got his plaid and stick.
"There! there's no danger of my finding

out her secret; I'm away to Allendale, and shan't be back till dark. Good-bye, my wee pet!" He looked for one moment at the beautiful child, standing there in the glow of the fire, her golden hair tossed about her rosy face, and the blue eyes still brimming over with fun; then, as if by an irresistible impulse, he turned back and laid his hand upon her head. " May God bless the bairn!" he said, and then turned and left the house. Truly his heart was bound up in the child!

Bonnie Bell waited till he was gone, and till old Jenny Kindred had cleared away the dinner-things, and adjourned to the byre to milk the new-calved cow; then she took down a little tin can, removed the lid, poured in her basin of broth, and put it on again, laughing softly to herself as she did so. "Puir auld John Armstrong! he's ill, and he'll like a wee sup broth; I'll tell daddy when I come back, and he'll not scold me, I ken that. He mightn't let me go if I told him first, ye ken; for he hasna forgiven Davie yet. Puir Davie! I doubt he'll hae thought me unkind to bide away sae lang. Won't he be glad when he sees me, though!" She laughed softly, bounded upstairs and donned her little cloak and hood, bounded down again, slipped her feet into her dainty spring-clogs, and clasped the shining buckles over her warm grey stockings. Then she took the bright tin can on her arm, whistled to Chevy, and, reaching up on tip-toe, unlatched the door and sallied forth.

It was February again, a cold grey day, like that on which we first made Davie's acquaintance, the year before. There was not so much wind, however, as there had been then, though it was not a whit less cold—a little cruel bitter wind, which had nothing grand or mighty about it, but which was very pertinacious, notwithstanding; creeping in at every chink of clothing, and giving spiteful little nips, and moaning, moaning, ceaselessly moaning like a fretful

elf. Bonnie Bell did not mind it much, however, with her warm little heart intent on an act of kindness, (though I will not say that she was quite right to go without her father's knowledge; but she did not think of that, poor child, how should she, when her will was always law?) and her merry spirits bubbling up like a mountain spring, making her dance up the road, till the shaking of the broth in her can warned her that a steadier pace would be more appropriate under the circumstances. " Now Isabella, this winna do," she said to herself, " ye'll have a' the broth spilt, 'or' ever it finds its way down auld John's throat. Steady, lass ! " As for Chevy, *she* did not mind the wicked little wind, not a bit of it; her fine shaggy coat kept it out very effectually, and she scampered about and jumped and barked in the joy of her heart, enough to keep any dog, that has not been spoilt by coddling, as warm as a toast. But it was a long walk to old Armstrong's cottage, longer

than Bonnie Bell had thought for ; and by
the time they had turned into the sheep
track, which led by a short cut across the
fells, the little feet had become rather weary,
and did not trip along at such a brisk pace
as before. The warmth of body, also, with
which she had left home, began to cool
down ; and the spiteful little wind, as if it
knew it well, renewed its attacks vehemently,
and succeeded in creeping in under the
duffle cloak. The child shivered now and
then, but she did not give in, that brave
little spirit, and, tired and cold though she
was beginning to be, pressed steadily onwards.
" Auld John must have his broth," she murmured, " I winna turn back." Chevy, too,
seemed to be settling down into a more
sober mood, for she left off her pranks and
jumping, and trotted quietly by her little
mistress's side, along the little brown track,
which threaded the great dreary waste of
withered heather and black peat-bogs.

" Chevy, Chevy, how dark it's getting ! "

said the child presently ; " I wonder if it's tea-time at home. What *will* old Jenny say when she canna find me ! Oh, it's a lang, lang, weary way ! isn't it, Chevy ? " Chevy looked up in her mistress's face, and gave a little whine, and the child shivered again. " Dinna whine, Chevy," she said, half petulantly, " I dinna like't. Oh, how dark it's gettin' ! it must be very late." It *was* getting dark, but not through the lateness of the hour, for it was not more than three o'clock. A dense curtain was slowly shutting out the daylight, dropping by degrees in heavy folds around the child and dog—the only figures on that lone, dark moor—creeping slowly, steadily along the waste, and hiding foot by foot of withered heather, till it finally threw off all disguise and showed itself for what it was—a heavy snow-storm. Still the child struggled on, though the bewildering cloud of snow-flakes fell thick and fast around her, for the little brown path still stretched on in front, like a

thread of hope to guide her through the
wilderness; but presently even that faint
clue was gone, the tiny track disappeared by
degrees, and all around became one great
white bewilderment, with only a black peat-
bog yawning here and there, like graves
beneath that ghastly pall, into which the
little feet stumbled many a time in the
gloom.

But Bonnie Bell was a mountain child,
and her spirit was not soon quelled; she
scrambled out, shook the black peat-earth
and the white snow-flakes from her damp
garments, and pressed on again, with Chevy
trotting steadily by her side. Now and then
they passed a knot of frightened sheep, hud-
dled closely together, under shelter of a great
block of limestone rock, which had fallen
from the heights above, and lay half em-
bedded in the soft soil; some among them
bore Thomas Reed's big red " T. R." stamped
on their wool, and at these good Chevy looked
wistfully, well knowing that they were her

charge, and that it was high time they were
driven to the home shelter; but the little
mistress called her, and she was fain to follow,
for the wise creature knew right well that
she was a more precious charge than a
hundred sheep. Faster and faster fell the
snow-flakes, more and more bewildering grew
the ever-whitening moor, and slower, more
weary became the child's footsteps, till at
length she stood still in utter bewilderment.
"Oh, Chevy, Chevy! where are we? I
canna see the way!" moaned the little one,
while tears dimmed the blue eyes, and
dropped upon the snow; but Chevy's soft
nose was poked into her hand, and once more
rallying her forces, Bonnie Bell gulped down
her tears, and struggled on through the ever-
thickening snow—struggled on till despair
had laid its cold hand on the little warm
heart, and weariness had utterly vanquished
the failing limbs, then the little feet refused
to move any more, and the child sank
exhausted on the cold snow, and burst into a

I

piteous wail—"Oh daddy, daddy! do come,
I'm so cold!" The brave little spirit broke
down completely, the tears rolled down her
cheeks, and her tiny form shook with sobs. It
was a sad sight, a heartrending sight; Chevy
seemed to feel it so, for she broke into
another long howl; but Bonnie Bell did not
heed her this time, she had grown exhausted
with sobbing, and was fast sinking into the
fatal stupor of cold. Suddenly she roused
herself,—"Oh, I'm going to sleep, and I
havena said my prayers!" she murmured,
half wandering already, but with the old
habit strong upon her; and raising herself
with difficulty, she knelt down and put her
tiny cold hands together. "Our Father!"
she whispered; but at that Name the thought
of her earthly father returned upon the poor
child with overwhelming force, and the rest
of the petitions were sobbed out, rather than
said. The deadly torpor was fast stealing over
her again, and the final prayer came from the
little blue lips with scarcely a sound,—

"'Gentle Jesus, meek and mild,
  Look upon a little child ;
  Pity my simplicity,
  And give me grace to come to Thee.
                              Amen.'"

The child sank down again, sobbing very
feebly now : a merciful sleep was falling upon
her, and fast numbing all sense of pain..

That last prayer was being answered; He
who has promised to gather the lambs with His
arm, and carry them in His bosom, He the
Good Shepherd was there in unseen presence
to guard His lost little one, and to shield her
from greater suffering than she could bear.
"Chevy, Chevy," murmured the child, "where
are you? Chevy, Chevy, dinna go away, bide
wi' me. Good night, daddy!" The dog
crept to her, and with a wise, affectionate
instinct, stretched herself on the child's
body; one little arm stole round the shaggy
neck, and a cold hand nestled in the silky
hair; then little Bonnie Bell did not move
any more, but her eyes closed, and there was
silence all around, broken only by the low

moan of the wintry wind, as it swept over
the moor, wailing piteously, as if remorseful
for what it had done. And still the snow-
flakes fell softly, silently, covering up the
little body, as the robins did those of the
babes in the wood; and the dog lay faithful
to her trust, with her soft brown eyes
watching for the help that came not.

*　　*　　*　　*　　*　　*

Time passed on—seconds, minutes, hours,
but there was none there to count them; the
snow-flakes got tired of falling, the snow-
clouds rolled slowly away, for their work was
done, and the sky was being swept and
garnished. One by one every vapour disappeared from the sapphire dome, and it hung
in deep stainless blue over the white spotless
earth. The stars came out above, and
with their tender golden eyes called forth
a responsive glitter from the snow beneath;
and the moon shone out on high, pure and
passionless, God's faithful witness in heaven
of the doings on earth—and still the child

slept on. And the cruel little wind, moaning with sorrow, tried to make reparation, by building up little walls of snow round her resting-place, in tiny crisp wavelets of powdered crystal, till the whole surface of the moor glittered like a frozen sea. And still the noble dog lay at her post, the only living creature in the wilderness,—watching, waiting for the help that tarried yet.

CHAPTER X.

A WARM peat fire burnt in the Armstrongs'
cottage that cold winter's night, for the old
man lay in his bed crippled with rheumatism, and the neighbours, with that kind
neighbourly feeling, which shows itself so
strongly in the "cannie North countrie,"
would not let him want for fuel, while peat
was to be had for the digging on their allot-
ments. So, in spite of the snow and wind
without, the little cottage was warm and
cosy enough. The old woman was seated in
her arm-chair, on one side of the fire, knitting a grey worsted stocking, and murmuring
plaintively to herself, according to custom;
while Davie sat on a cracket (*a low wooden*

stool) at the other, in moody silence, with
his hands stretched out to the glow. That
moody silence was growing on the boy; since
his last fall, he seemed to have lost all hope
of ever becoming better, and, though he had
not since committed any grave sin, he had
allowed the reins to slip looser and looser,
and was fast falling into that state of callous
recklessness, which is ready to yield without
a struggle on the slightest temptation, and
plunge into open sin, careless of consequences,
both in this world and the next. God have
mercy on the lad, it would require a terrible
punishment to rouse him now!

Silence had reigned for some time in the
cottage-room, unbroken save by the murmur
of the old woman's voice and the clicking of
her needles,—for even the asthmatic old clock
was gone now,—when there came a shuffling
outside, as of feet coming through the deep
snow, and then a loud knock at the door.
Davie started up and opened it, and a man
entered, muffled in a big grey plaid, whom

Davie recognised for one of the small statesmen of Ayle. " I say, David Armstrong,
have ye got Tam Reed's wee dowter here?"
Davie stared at him. " Tam Reed's dowter !"
he exclaimed; " no, I havena spoken to her
since summer." "Well," said the man, "she's
missin'; and Jenny Kindred she thought she
just might hae come here, hearin' the auld
man was badly ; for she's ta'en the wee can wi'
a few broth along wi' her. So ye've not seen
her ?" Davie turned very pale. " No," was
all he could say. " Eh, folks !" exclaimed
the man, "here's a bonnie look-out! Tam
Reed awa', and the bairn missin' sin' two
o'clock, and sich a storm as there's been !
Jenny Kindred never missed her till tea-
time; she thought she was in ane · o' the
neighbour's houses. Lord hae mercy on the
bairn ! It'd break Tam Reed's heart to lose
her."

While the man was speaking, Davie had
rushed to the peg, taken down his plaid, and
flung it hastily around him, seized his cap

and stick, whistled to Laddie, and was pushing past him out of the door. "Where are ye off to, David, mon?" "I'm awa' to seek t' bairn." "Ou, aye," answered the other, "though there isna mickle (*much*) chance o' findin' her alive, puir wee lassie! We'd better go different ways, so as—— Why, hinnies me, the lad's off!" Yes, Davie was already quite out of hearing, and was rushing almost frantically through the deep snow, which was still falling in heavy flakes. A terrible fear was goading him on. What if that sweet little child should be cut off, in the bright morning of her youth, and through his fault? Yes, it was this thought which tortured the boy, in his agony of suspense and fear, making him wander aimlessly over the moor, calling on her name, now wildly, now imploringly, "Bonnie Bell! *Bonnie Bell!*" But there was neither voice nor answer. Long did he wander there, up and down, all over those white cold fells; going over the ground again and again, till he almost began to hope she was not there, after all. The storm was over, the moon shone out, making it almost as light as day, and still he found her not.

Suddenly his dog sprang forward, stopped at a little hillock of snow, and began to scratch it violently with his paws. Davie's heart sank; he followed the dog, and there, still half-buried in the snow, lay wee Bonnie Bell, stiff and cold, with Chevy still stretched upon her, in the vain endeavour to keep her warm. Poor Chevy, faithful Chevy, it would soon have been all over with her, too; she had just strength left to lick Davie's hand, as he lifted the child in his arms, and to drag herself painfully after him over the snow. And Davie?—I can scarcely tell you how it was with him, as he carried the senseless body of his little friend to her desolated home. When he looked at that still, white face, a dreadful conviction struck him that all was over; life was gone, and with it hope, and the awe of death fell upon him, making.

him very quiet in his dumb despair. He reached the village, walked up to the house-door, and knocked. Old Jenny opened it hurriedly, then started back horror-stricken. "Eh, dear heart, dear heart!" she sobbed wildly, "my bairn, my bairn! Gi'e her here, lad, canna ye?" The old woman took the child in her arms, sat down in a low chair, and rocked herself backwards and forwards, moaning, "Oh, my lamb, my lamb, my wee bonnie lamb! Oh, wae's me!" Suddenly she jumped up, and hurried into the inner room. " Lasses, lasses, let's see if we canna bring her round. It *canna* be she's dead, the sweet wee thing! Eh, mercy me! what'll t' maister do?"

The room was by this time full of the feminine population of the village, and no sooner did old Jenny talk of trying restoratives, than there was a general rush, one for the kettle, another for hot flannels, and a third for brandy. " Eh, dear, it's nae use, nae use!" murmured an old woman, wiping her eyes

with her apron. "Nae use, I doubt," cried
a younger and more energetic matron; "but
we can but try, woman! Eh, folks! what
does a lad want here?" she exclaimed, nearly
tumbling over Davie, as she hurried past with
a kettle of hot water; "a man body can do
nae good, at sich a time. Move out o' t'
way, lad!" Davie turned away silently, sub-
missively, and left the house without a word.
Poor lad, he was completely stunned at the
time, but terrible was the agony when his
faculties began to awaken once more. In his
anguish of morbid remorse, it seemed to him
that Bonnie Bell's death (for he had scarcely
a hope that she would recover) rested on his
head. As is usually the case, in his passionate
repentance, he saw his sins in an exaggerated
light, and thus he magnified his share in the
terrible misfortune which had happened. I
say he magnified his guilt, for I cannot think
that he was clear in the matter. If it had
not been for his sin, he would not have had
to leave Thomas Reed's service, and thus little

Bonnie Bell would never have undertaken
that walk to the distant cottage over the hill.
So true is it, that we cannot sin without
bringing sorrow on others as well as ourselves.
Poor Davie! sharp was his punishment, and
bitter, oh! so bitter his repentance. All that
night long he knelt in his loft, with his arms
leaning on the bed, and his face buried
between them; never moving, never feeling
the cold, saying no prayer but those old, old
words uttered long ago by a penitent, humbled
to the dust as he was,—" God be merciful to
me a sinner !"

CHAPTER XI.

ONE LITTLE EWE LAMB.

In the meantime, all was hurry and bustle
at the farm-house. The doctor had been sent
for, but no time was lost in waiting for him.
The child was laid on the bed in the inner
room and carefully undressed. Jenny, now
fully restored to her presence of mind by the
exigencies of the case, stood by the bed-side
trying to force a spoonful of hot brandy and
water between the little blue lips, while others
chafed the icy hands and feet. Not far from
the bed crouched faithful Chevy, with her
brown eyes still fixed on the child she had
done her best to save, quite unnoticed by the
hurrying crowd of women, whose anxious
voices and quick contradictory commands
made an unwonted hum in the usually quiet

house, where lights flashed from the windows as they were carried from room to room, making strange gleams on the snow without, and mingling wierdly with the moonlight.

"Dost see any signs of life, Jenny?" asked one woman, stooping anxiously over the little still form. "Eh, woman, I believe I see'd her lips move! Quick, some more brandy!" Then there was a fresh hurrying to and fro; but the child still lay white, stiff, and motionless, fast locked in that mysterious sleep, which had fallen upon her on the wild moor. Would she *never* awake again? Old Jenny's heart began to ask itself that question, as she bent over her darling, trying not to despair, hoping against hope; but her tones ever growing sharper, her voice more confident, as those of her neighbours grew less so. "Eh, dear, I fear it's nae use, nae use!" murmured the desponding dame again, and this time her more hopeful gossip did not contradict her, but turned away with a tear in her kindly eye.

It was at this moment that horse's hoofs
were heard without, falling softly in the snow
that lay deep over the village street. "Will
it be the doctor, think ye?" asked a neighbour
quickly. Jenny did not answer directly, she
was listening intently. The horse stopped
before the house, and was immediately led
away to the stable. "Eh, no, it'll be t'
master," whispered the old housekeeper, in
an awe-stricken tone. "Eh, dear, how *will* I
tell him?" None of her companions were
prepared to answer this question; a sudden
hush fell upon them, for all feared to tell the
father how it was with his own little daughter.
They listened, trembling. There was a clink-
ing sound in the adjoining stable, as the bit
and saddle were taken off, and thrown down in
a corner to wait for daylight to be put away.
Then a little moving about; the farmer was
fastening up and foddering his horse. A
moment more, the stable-door shut, and steps
came through the deep snow, and stopped
before the house door. The women held their

breath with fear. Then there came a knocking and shuffling, as the snow was shaken
from the heavy shoes, after which the door
opened, and Thomas Reed appeared on the
threshold, looking in amazement at the unwonted guests who thronged his kitchen.

"What's all this?" he asked, in a voice
half angry, half surprised. No one answered;
the women glanced at each other, no one
would be the first to speak. With the quick
instinct of love, the father's thoughts turned
to his child. "Where's the bairn?" he asked
in a voice sharp with undefined dread.
"Where's the bairn?" he repeated; as no
one replied, " Mrs. Wood, canna ye answer a
man?" Thus peremptorily called upon, the
woman came forward, and her tongue once
set free, burst into a long confused history.
" 'Deed, Mr. Reed, and I'm sorry for ye, I am.
It's a sore thing for a father when any ill
comes to his only bairn, it is that. But ye
can blame naebody, I'm sure; the bairn was
wilful, puir wee lassie, and used to gang her

K

ain gait (*take her own way*), and wha can
blame her either, puir lamb! situated as she
was, with never a mother to look to her?
And in sich a storm as there's been! And
sae far off as the Armstrongs' is! It's nae
wonder it should ha' happened; it's only
unco' strange she should ha' been found at
all, it is; and by auld John's Davie too!
Puir lassie, they say it was to tak' the auld
man a few broth she went. Eh, dear, dear!
it is sad, it is. But I *will* say——'' What
she would have said I cannot tell, for Reed
having gathered enough to fill him with a
fearful dread, turned impatiently away, and
entered the inner room.

The sight which met him there was too
much; he turned deadly pale, staggered
against the door, and covered his face with
his hands. The occupants of the outer room
stole softly away; the master was home, and
they knew they were not wanted, and all now
believed that there was no more that they
could do. One by one they left the house,

and returned sorrowfully to their own homes,
leaving old Jenny alone, with the father and
child. Reed stood motionless till the last was
gone, and then, as though incapable of any
further self-control, he fell on his knees by
the bed-side, and covering his face, the pent-
up agony of the father's heart burst forth.
It was a fearful sight to see that strong man,
bowed down by grief, trembling and sobbing
like a little child, calling on the lifeless form
to awake, in appealing piteous accents, and
then breaking down, and groaning in the
anguish of despair,—"Oh, Bonnie Bell, my
bairn, my bairn! my sweet wee thing, speak
to me; do not leave your old daddy without
a word! Oh God, she winna hear! It was
cruel, cruel to tak' her, my only one—— But
no, what am I sayin'? It was just, it is a
judgment upon me—justice wi'out mercy,
like that I showed the lad. He offended and
I would not forgive, I would not hear when he
spoke, and now this has come upon me.
Does not the Bible say, 'With what measure

ye mete, it shall be measured to you again?"
Yes, that is it; but, oh God, it is bitter,
bitter! But it *canna* be, she canna be *quite*
gone. Bonnie Bell, Bonnie Bell, my bairn,
my bairn!"

What was it? Was it that the force of that
strong, great love had power to call back
a soul hovering on the verge of eternity?
Who can say? God is more merciful than
men; but at that bitter imploring cry, the
charmed sleep was broken, the blue eyes
opened. "Master, master!" cried old Jenny,
trembling with excitement, as she touched
her master's shoulder, "dear heart, dinna
tak' on sae, she's comin' round, the Lord be
thanked! Now for another spoonful o'
speerits,—Eh, dear, this *is* a mercy!" And
so it was. This time the restoratives proved
successful, and God gave back to the father
the life of his only child, of his one little ewe
lamb.

CHAPTER XII.

"DADDY!" Thomas Reed looked up from his station by his child's bed, from whence he had scarcely stirred during the whole of the afternoon following the day of the storm. Old Jenny was busy in the kitchen, and he had been watching the quiet breathing of his little daughter as she lay in the long blessed sleep from which she had not awakened that day. He had been thinking much— deeply, as he sat there, thinking over his past life, 'a decent, respectable life, people would have called it, for he had gone to church pretty regularly, and had always stood well in the eyes of the world, but he had recked little of higher things,—he had not drawn near to God in the days when all went well, and, but for this great shock, he might never have awakened from his sleep of false security. But God had been merciful to him; the sore fear and the great relief had stirred the still waters of the man's soul to their very depths, and as he sat there watching, many thoughts had passed through his mind,— thoughts which had brought the unaccustomed moisture more than once into his deepset grey eyes. He now looked up, at the sound of his little daughter's voice, and met her blue eyes fixed upon him, with a look of full, quiet recognition, a look he had never thought to see there again, when he gazed upon her the night before. "What is it, my bairnie?" he asked, bending over her, and softening his loud, bluff tones to their gentlest.

"Daddy, what's been the matter? Why am I in bed? surely it's terrible late. Oh, daddy, I've had such a fearfu' dream! I thought the cauld white snow had quite covered me up, and I should never, never see

my daddy again. Oh, it was horrible!" She
shivered as she spoke, and nestled up nearer
to her father. "Never mind, my wee lassie,"
he said coaxingly, "it's a' over now; daddy'ill
never let ye get lost again. But what did
ye run away for, my bit bairnie? Ye mustn't
go for to leave daddy that way, any more."
"Then it wasna a dream? It was a' true?
Oh, daddy, ye mauna be angry wi' me! I
wanted to take the broth to puir auld John
Armstrong; he's vara ill, ye ken, and I thought
ye'd not mind. Ye're not angry wi' me,
daddy?" "*Angry*, my bonnie lassie? What call
have I to be angry, when my little bairn was
set on mending her father's fault? But she'll
not go away again without tellin' her daddy,
will she? What would puir old daddy do,
if he lost his Bonnie Bell?" The man's
voice choked as he said this; he could scarcely
bear to think about what *might* have been.
Bonnie Bell looked at her father with wonder
in her wide blue eyes, then she said gravely,
"No, daddy, I winna do't any more." There

was silence for a few minutes; then she spoke again, "Where's Chevy? She was *so* kind in the snow. Daddy, I want to thank her." Reed rose, opened the door, and called "Chevy!" and with a bound of delight, the dog sprang in; she had been lying there, waiting patiently on the threshold. You may imagine that the meeting between Chevy and her little mistress was of the warmest nature. The dog was almost wild with joy, and bounded and leaped about in such an outrageous fashion, that Reed wished to banish her again, but Bonnie Bell would not hear of that, and the matter was compromised at length by Chevy taking up her station on the bed, to the no small detriment of old Jenny's clean counterpane, where she calmed down, and lay gently licking her little mistress's hand from time to time, as though to make sure that she was all safe.

When Bonnie Bell next spoke, it was to ask who had brought her home. " Who d'ye think?" asked Reed, in a tone which tried hard not to appear disturbed. "Why, your friend David Armstrong." "Oh, daddy, I'm so glad! And ye'll forgi'e him now, won't ye? He saved me, ye ken, daddy;" and she looked up coaxingly into her father's face. Little rogue, she knew her power, and the force this last argument would have. The moisture came again into his eyes, and as he passed his hand hastily over them, his voice grew husky with something that was certainly not anger. "As I hope to be forgiven, my bairn," was the solemn answer. The child was awed by her father's look, but it soon passed, and then she was all eagerness that he should go and fetch Davie. "I must thank him, ye ken, daddy. Oh, I'm so happy, now it's a' right and we shall a' be friends again! But ye'll go for Davie, daddy?" "Aye, aye, little woman," answered Reed, and he got up and left the room. He had not far to seek; the minute he opened the house-door, he saw Davie standing near, irresolute whether to come up or not. A scarlet flush rose to the lad's face on perceiving his former master, and he would have turned hastily away, had not Reed called out to him in a voice that was at once kindly and constrained, "Come here, lad; dost want anything?" Poor Davie flushed hotter than ever, for he felt as though caught where he had no right to be; he had no choice, however, but to come forward.

"Please, sir, I beg pardon, but I did so want to ken how she is," he faltered. The rough farmer was touched so as almost to forget his embarrassment. He laid his hand on the boy's shoulder. " Come in and see her, lad; ye've a right to, if anybody has. If it hadna been for ye last night——" the farmer coughed and broke short off, then began again hurriedly, " We'll make it up, won't we, Davie?" He held out his hand. Davie took it eagerly, but his voice was so choked, he could hardly speak. "I *am* sorry, sir," he began. "I——" The farmer interrupted him hastily. " That's right, Davie lad; now we're

a' friends again, as the little lass' says.
Come your ways in." And so that great
punishment had been spared him. This was
what Davie was thinking of, as with a very
full heart he followed Reed into the tidy
little bed-room, and saw the child's head
lying on its white pillow, all framed about
by the dark oak of the box-bed; the wet
golden hair all bright and dry again, a faint
pink colour tinging the cheek which had
lain on his shoulder last night, so deadly pale,
and the life-light back again in the blue
eyes which he had thought would never
open more on earth. And yet, in his great
joy, Davie was very shy; it seemed so strange
to be in that house again, and to be treated
by both father and daughter more kindly
even, than if nothing had happened. It was
too much, he could not feel comfortable under
it all, his voice quivered strangely whenever he spoke, and finally, when Bonnie
Bell asked after his grandfather, a great sob
rose in his throat, and he was obliged to

turn away his head a moment before he answered, "Oh, he's—he's very badly; the doctor says he's failin' fast;" then the tears broke out, and the lad covered his face with his hands. Reed got up, and with an innate delicacy of feeling, left the boy alone with the child; he felt they would do best together. Bonnie Bell let him be for a while, then she put out her little soft hand and stroked his, murmuring in a little coaxing voice, as she had done on the hill-side, "Poor Davie, I'm so sorry; don't cry, please don't!" "But it's my fault, I know it is," sobbed the poor lad; "he went out one night, to get the sheep in for me, when I wasna there, and he got wet, and ever syne (*since*) he's been worse. He's been sae badly of late, that he couldna speak, and I'm afraid he'll die, and never be able to say he forgie's me." "Oh no, Davie, I dinna think that: I'll ask God for ye, Davie," she added in a very low voice, "only dinna cry, Davie; please, *please* don't, I canna bide it." The little voice

trembled, and the blue eyes filled too. Davie
saw he was distressing the child, and made
a great effort to recover himself. "Well, I
won't, then. Good-bye, Bonnie Bell; I hope
I'll find ye nicely when I come again." He
rose to go. "Good-bye, Davie; ye'll come
back again soon? We're a' friends again
now, ye ken." The sunshine came back to
her sweet face, and she put up her mouth to
be kissed. Davie stooped down and kissed
the wee cherry lips, though it almost made
him break down again; but, as he walked
home, little Bonnie Bell's words kept sounding
in his ears, like a prophecy of future, as well
as present comfort,—" We're a' friends again
now."

CHAPTER XIII.

OLD ARMSTRONG'S LAST WORDS.

YES, old John Armstrong was failing fast. All through the slowly-lengthening days, when the colour was coming back to the child's cheeks and the strength to her limbs, the old man lay in a half torpid state, scarcely conscious, drifting slowly away towards the sea of eternity. But it was not a thing for bitter grief, as the death of the child would have been; no, the old man's decline was very peaceful; ripe for the Reaper's hand, wearied with the burden and heat of the day, he lay waiting calmly till the call of his Lord should come. Something of his quietness seemed to have fallen upon the two watchers. The old woman's peevish murmuring was

stilled, she moved softly about, waiting on
him carefully; or sat at her knitting, with
her eyes fixed on the aged face of her husband,
so calm in sleep, so happy-looking, that
noisy lamentations would have seemed all
out of place.   And Davie, too, was very quiet,
doing all he could think of for his grandfather,
and quite surprising his grandmother by his
changed ways and ever-ready help.   It
seemed as though the lad were striving to
make up, in those few short days, for all the
trouble he had caused the old man during
the many years.   It seemed so to others; but
to Davie, all he could do was as nothing,
and the lad's heart knew its own bitterness;
quieted, kept down before others, or when
there was anything to do; but when all was
done and he was alone, it was very sore to
bear.

There was no want now in the little
cottage; everything that could be needed
was supplied from the farm; and Reed and
Bonnie Bell might constantly be seen coming

of an evening, after work was over, with a little can of soup, a jug of new milk, or anything they thought old Armstrong might fancy. The Rector, too, came regularly; but Davie was still very shy, and got out of the way, whenever he saw him coming. So things went on. At last, about a fortnight after the day when little Bonnie Bell had so nearly lost her life, there came an evening when Davie was sitting alone watching by his grandfather's bed. Mrs. Armstrong had gone to Ayle, on an errand to the Reeds, and quietness had it all its own way in the little cottage. It was a calm mild evening, and Davie had set the window ajar, to cool the heated atmosphere of the small room. A sweet breath of fresh air stole in at the opening, fragrant of wet earth from the little garden, where the currant-bushes were beginning to put forth little tightly-cased pink buds, which promised green leaves by-and-by; and where the snowdrops were shaking out their pure white bells, by ones and twos in

the neglected borders.   A red-breasted robin
was swinging airily on a branch of the old fir-
trees, singing his sweet little song, the last
time, perhaps, that it would be much noticed,
for the season was almost over, and he would
soon have to retire and give place to singers
of greater distinction.   And Davie sat there
in the stillness, watching the gentle old face
which lay so calmly on the pillow, and longing, longing in vain that the days which
were gone might but come over again.   How
is it that we never think of *that* till it is too
late?   " If he would only speak to me once
more !"   murmured the lad, half aloud ; " if
I might but hear him say he forgives me,
afore——" He stopped suddenly; the old
man's eyes were wide open, and were resting upon him with a look full of gentle-
ness and love, and the trembling lips which
had not spoken for days, were moving with a
faint sound.   The lad drew nearer, bent over
the bed, and heard his own name,—"Davie!"
" Yes, dear grandfather; did ye want any-

L

thing?" "Davie," said the old man again,
more distinctly, "come nigher." The lad
knelt down by the bed and put his head close
to that of his grandfather. The feeble hand
was raised with difficulty, and rested heavily
on the boy's bent head. "God Almighty
bless the lad," murmured the aged voice
again, "God Almighty keep him, and grant
that he may take heed to the thing that is
lawful and right, for that only shall bring
a man peace at the last." "Grandfather,"
whispered Davie, in a voice awed and hushed
by the solemn scene, "grandfather, I'm so
sorry; can ye forgi'e me?" "May God
forgi'e ye, my ain bairn, even as I do!"
Then there was silence for some minutes.
"Davie," said the old man again, in a voice
so low that the lad could scarce hear,—
"Davie, say it,—Our Father——" "Our
Father which art in heaven," replied the boy
in a calm steady voice, "hallowed be Thy
Name. Thy kingdom come. Thy will be
done in earth, as it is in heaven. Give us

this day our daily bread. And forgive us
our trespasses, as we forgive them that tres-
pass against us.   And lead us not into temptation : but deliver us from evil : for Thine
is the kingdom, the power, and the glory, for
ever and ever. Amen."   A light broke on
the old man's face. "Even for ever and ever!"
he whispered. They were the last words old
John Armstrong spoke.

CHAPTER XIV.

PARDON AND PEACE.

THE morning of the funeral came in, tearful yet bright,—one of those days one often finds towards the end of February, which seem like a foretaste of the spring, while it is yet afar off. The snow had melted away, with the exception of a patch or two behind the stone dykes, and some long white streaks which lingered in the furrows of the hills. There was an expectant flutter in the yet leafless branches of the trees, where the blackbirds were beginning to tune their throats, letting fall a note or two, and then stopping, as though uncertain whether or not the time of the singing-birds were come;

and the sky seemed just as uncertain as the blackbirds, for now a few drops of rain would fall, and then the sun would shine out brightly and cheerfully, as though it did not know whether to smile or cry. Truly it was a day of hope, a herald of the coming spring, and still further a type of the glorious Resurrection, when the dead shall rise again, and we shall be changed. As the appointed hour approached, the mourners began to assemble; and when all had arrived, the coffin was carried out, and placed on chairs before the door, where, according to the ancient and beautiful custom of the country, the mourners grouped themselves around it and sung a hymn. Sweetly it rose into the quiet air, though the music was quaint, and the voices untrained :—

> "The Lord Himself, the mighty Lord,
> Vouchsafes to be my guide;
> The Shepherd by whose constant care
> My wants are all supplied.

In tender grass He makes me feed,
    And gently there repose ;
Then leads me to cool shades, and where
    Refreshing water flows.

He does my wandering soul reclaim,
    And to His endless praise,
Instruct with humble zeal to walk
    In His most righteous ways.

I pass the gloomy vale of Death,
    From fear and danger free ;
For there His aiding rod and staff
    Defend and comfort me.

Since God does thus His wondrous love
    Through all my life extend,
May I that life to him devote,
    And in His service spend ! "

The widow and fatherless thought of the
Valley of the Shadow, and sobbed drearily ;
but as the last tones of the hymn died away,
the blackbirds took up the song, and in their
notes was the sweet sound of hope, for they
seemed to say,—" Behold He careth for the
birds of the air, and shall He not much more
care for you, O ye of little faith ? "   Then

four tall mountaineers took up the coffin, and bore it on their shoulders along the rough fell road, that the feet of him whom they were carrying to his last resting-place had so often trod in life. But he recked little of it, for can we doubt but that that good old man was already in the Paradise of God, resting from the labours of his long life, and tasting of that joy unspeakable which endureth for ever and ever? It was a long company of mourners which wound along the hill-side that day, for old John Armstrong had been loved and reverenced by everybody, and his death was much felt. On nearing the church they began to sing again, and as the concluding notes died away among the echoes, the white-robed Priest of the Most High met the train with the salutation, so solemn and yet so full of hope,—" I am the Resurrection and the Life, saith the Lord: he that believeth in Me, though he were dead, yet shall he live: and whosoever liveth and believeth in Me shall never die."

"I know that my Redeemer liveth." The
solemn service was over, the grave was filled
in, and the mourners turned away, leading
the old woman with them, for she was
stunned and bewildered with grief, and pas-
sive as a child. The evergreen boughs of
the fir-trees swayed in the breeze, casting
flickering shadows over the green mounds
and grey headstones of the little churchyard
among the hills, and the sweet hopeful sunbeams basked lovingly on the new-made grave,
where no grass grew as yet, and friends and
kinsfolk had taken their last look, and were
gone out one by one, leaving the little bury-
ing-ground to silence. Yet one still knelt
by the new-made grave, as though all his
love and hope on earth were hidden away
there. Poor Davie! perhaps his had been
the most hopelessly sorrowful heart in that
funeral train, and now that all were gone,
he had remained by the grave, longing,
yearning for one more sound of the gentle
voice which he had so little heeded till it

was silenced in this world for ever. Poor
lad, he was brought very low, but a better
time was coming. Davie still knelt by the
grave, so lost to all around that he had
not heard a step coming over the grass,
and it was only when a hand was laid
upon his shoulder that he looked up, and
with a start and a rush of colour, beheld
the Rector.

I am not going to tell you what was said
there by the new-made grave, but I think
you may guess pretty well by the look on
Davie's face, when, after the Rector had
placed his hand on his head, and promised
him pardon for his sins in the name of God,
he turned his steps homewards. The hope-
less, despairing look was no longer there, but
in its place had come another, sad indeed and
sorrowing still, but full of steadfast trusting
hope, as of one who would strive in the strength
of a Higher than he, resting in the merits of
Him who died to save us from our sins.
Surely there was joy in the presence of the

angels of God, as over one sinner that
repenteth.

*   *   *   *   *   *

It is on a bright Easter-day, still in that
same spring, that we bid farewell to our
friend Davie. The greater part of the congregation have come out of church, but a
little band of faithful ones remain there to
receive the Holy Communion, and among
them, for the first time, is kneeling David Armstrong, by the side of one who has long been
a stranger there, old Thomas Reed. Outside
in the church-yard the spring wind is whispering in the trees, gladdening them with
soft promises of coming leaves, and the blackbirds are plucking up their courage, and
whistling with more confidence in their clear
notes, while the river keeps up a running accompaniment as it flows past, swollen with
the melted snow, of which it is fast robbing
old white-capped Cross Fell. And the spring
sun looks down on the green graves, making

them greener with his smile of hope, faintly foreshadowing what shall be, when the Sun of Righteousness shall arise with healing on His wings, and the dead shall come forth in shining apparel to meet their risen Lord. Tender grass is already beginning to spring on old John Armstrong's grave, where a simple headstone, the gift of Thomas Reed, records his name, and the date of his death.

The service is over; the congregation leave the church quietly and reverently, and pass down the church-yard path. Presently Davie comes out and pauses by his grandfather's grave. The steadfast look is still on his face, deepened and strengthened by the holy influence of that blessed Feast of which he has just been a partaker, and by which he has received strength from above to stand firm in the hour of temptation. Thomas Reed also comes out and joins him by the grave, and little Bonnie Bell, who has been waiting in another part of the church-yard, seeing her father, runs up to him and quietly puts her hand into his.

For some moments no one spoke; then the old farmer held out his hand. "Davie, lad," he blurted out, "I meant to ha' told ye long syne, but somehow I never could get it said; I'm sorry, lad, for havin' turned ye off sae hastily like; but I'm a peppery-tempered auld chap, and ye maun forgi'e me; God kens I was like to hae suffered for it." A suspicious glistening came into Reed's eyes, as he looked down at his child, and squeezed the little hand he held. Davie took the old man's proffered hand eagerly. "Oh, sir, dinna say that! it's a' my fault; I've been a bad lad, but I *am* sorry, and I mean to try and do better. I think—I think I ken how better now,—*she* told me first," he added in a low voice, looking lovingly at the pretty child, who stood listening with grave wonder in her blue eyes. "I'm going to part wi' my shepherd at May-day, and ye shall have the place again, lad," resumed Reed presently.

"Oh, thank ye, sir! I—I don't deserve——"
The lad broke down with a stifled sob, and
turned away his face. "Aye, aye, lad," answered the old man, "we none o' us deserve
God's mercies; we seldom think mickle (*much*)
o' His good gifts till He is like to take them
away. We have both thought over-little o'
these things, but He has sent us a merciful
reminder, in sparin' us a vara bitter sorrow.
Aye, lad, He was good to spare us the little
lass!" He put his hand lovingly on the
child's head, she looked up and smiled, and
slipped her other little hand into Davie's.
"Aye, aye, lad," continued the farmer, "I
shall never forget it, never as long as I live;
and I hope by God's grace we may both do
better in future, for it seems to me that He
has said to both of us to-day, 'Thy sins be
forgiven thee.'"

* * * * * *

The little whitewashed church which Davie
knew is no longer there; in its place has arisen

a beautiful little building, where God's faithful people may worship Him in the beauty of holiness. Among the green hills it stands, the slender spire of its arrow-headed belfry pointing upwards to where their tops rest against the blue heavens, reminding one of the words of the Psalmist:—

"I will lift up mine eyes unto the hills, from whence cometh my help."

CLARENDON PRESS, OXFORD.

FOR THE SOCIETY FOR PROMOTING CHRISTIAN KNOWLEDGE.